LACQUER & SILVER

LACQUER & SILVER

Oriental Elegance for Western Tables

FUMI KIMURA

Photographs by ICHIGO SUGAWARA

Kodansha International
Tokyo · New York · London

The author and the publisher would like to thank the following for their support:
International Hotel Kanazawa; Flower Shop Araki; Koshudo; Ito Shoyudo;
Eternal, Inc.; Lalique Japan Co., Ltd; Jane Dimmock; Hudson River Club; Goodwin Gallery;
Colette Rossant; Rainbow Room; Thanks International Corp.; Restaurant Nippon;
Kodansha America, Inc.; Tiffany & Co.; Meier Advertising, Inc.; Sasaki Glass Co., Ltd.;
Nikko Co.; Interrock Co., Ltd., Image Shop Omphalos; Grand Hyatt Hong Kong; Yokomasa Co., Ltd.;
Tazza Co., Ltd.; Hoya Corp.; Noritake Co., Ltd.; Fujin Gaho-sha; Kodansha Ltd.

Book design by Tomoko Nawata (L'espace Inc.)
Translated by Juliet Winters Carpenter
Additional photographs by Tetsuo Yuasa (pp. 110–111), Shiro Senba (p. 127), Yutaka Sato (p. 146, p. 152)
Line drawings by Mitsuru Iijima
Edited by Michiko Hiraoka
Additional text by Yoshiko Ikoma
Tablesetting coordination by Mayumi Yamamoto
Tablesetting assistance by Ikuko Maekawa, Hiromi Shinkai, Shinobu Yoshida, Yumiko Ichimura

Distributed in the United States by Kodansha America, Inc., 114 Fifth Avenue, New York, N.Y., 10011,
and in the United Kingdom and continental Europe by Kodansha Europe Ltd.,
Gillingham House, 38–44 Gillingham Street, London SW1V 1HU.
Published by Kodansha International Ltd., 17–14, Otowa 1-chome, Bunkyo-ku, Tokyo 112, and Kodansha America, Inc.

Printed in Japan by Dai Nippon Co., Ltd., Tokyo.

Library of Congress Cataloging-in-Publication Data
Kimura, Fumi. 1948–
Lacquer & silver: oriental elegance for western tables / Fumi Kimura:
photographs by Ichigo Sugawara.
    p.   cm.
1. Table setting and decoration.   2. Tableware.
I. Sugawara, Ichigo.   II. Title.   III. Title: Lacquer and silver.   IV. Title: Oriental elegance for western tables.
TX873. K56   1991
642' .6–dc20
CIP 91–21341
ISBN 4-7700-1577-1

First edition, 1991
91 92 93 94 10 9 8 7 6 5 4 3 2 1

PREFACE

The past few decades have seen countries all over the world begin to take interest in each other's cultures, resulting in increased cultural exchanges. I myself have learned much from Western countries and from the peoples of Asia. Through my involvement with various hotel and restaurant projects creating dining environments and tablesettings, I have had many opportunities to reconsider the cultural diversity of dining practices. At the same time, my interest as a Japanese in my native culture was rekindled. I thought how wonderful it would be to study the role of food and eating in the history of other countries, and to have the pleasure of expressing what I learned in my daily life. *Lacquer & Silver* is the result.

I have sought to design tablesettings in an eclectic, crossover style, from the viewpoint of Japanese functions, traditions and dining customs. The desire to entertain guests in a hospitable atmosphere exists in all countries. As an author, nothing would make me happier than if my readers found some inspiration from this book that they could then apply in their own entertaining occasions.

Nearly two and a half years have elapsed since this book entered the planning stage. I have a store of fond memories: at picture-taking sessions from New York to Hong Kong and Kanazawa, at all hours of the day and night, during which more people than I can name have offered their assistance. The challenges of the photography, and the privilege of meeting so many people, have been a source of excitement and joy that no one knows but my staff. And yet, to me the energy generated by all of these experiences seems to burst from each page in the book. It would please me immensely if readers could sense even a part of what has gone into creating these pages.

To each of my staff members, and to these who provided editorial assistance, I offer my heartfelt thanks.

CONTENTS

INTRODUCTION

When considering changing styles in dining, it seems evident that as we proceed into the 21st century, the emphasis will shift from dining *space* to total dining *environment*. The former refers to the actual physical space where the act of eating occurs, and includes furnishings, tableware, and lighting; the latter to the larger context of dining, including regional climate, history, and culture. Perhaps the major difference between space and environment is that one is easily movable, while the other is not. People have often noted that while it is perfectly possible to create a Tokyo branch of a Parisian café, for example, faithfully reproducing the original decor and menu, it is far more difficult, if not impossible, to recreate the identical atmosphere. That fact plainly reveals the limitations of attempts to transplant dining space alone, with no regard for dining environment.

As information and transportation networks continue to develop, and travel increases until society gradually loses its borders, cross-cultural enrichment and understanding will inevitably run deeper than ever before. In the realm of food and dining, there must be deeper awareness not only of the dining spaces of other cultures, but of their dining environments as well. In seeking to learn about the dining habits of people in a given region, we must not only study the shapes of utensils and the contents of dishes, but take a wideranging approach that embraces the region's cultural and geographical background, including the history of tableware and cooking, ceremonies and

 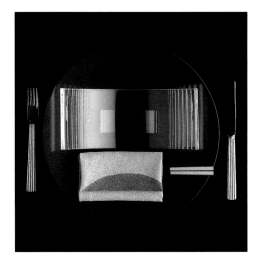

festivals, the history of architecture, the family, climate, and so on. To do so is to increase the pleasure of shared understanding as well.

The dining table is affected by regionality, by historical time, and by total cultural environment. Now we have the privilege and the pleasure of focusing on these various elements to blend them in harmonious ways, freely creating and enjoying the resulting new styles. If, through the act of dining, we can discover a new sense of beauty and a heightened appreciation of our blessings, then the time we devote to food can impart greater depth and meaning to our lives overall.

Let us begin with an explanation of the word "crossover" as used in this book. The meaning of the word goes beyond a simple sense of mixing East and West, or old and new, to include a more comprehensive synthesis in which time, place, and human sensibility mingle and blend, in all their rich complexity. This multi-faceted sense of crossover embodies the spirit of the times and can lead to the discovery of a new sense of beauty.

The crossover tablesetting perspective is based on three types of harmonious encounters. The first type is cross-cultural. Each

culture on earth has its own ways of selecting, arranging, and setting off tableware; combining and harmonizing these cultural approaches is the first condition of presenting a crossover sensibility on the table.

The second type of encounter involves being transported into a time other than the present. From ancient times to the present, each era has nurtured its own dietary culture, and devised its own ways of serving food. To mix elements from different time frames, and thereby create a refreshing and beautiful harmony, is another important aspect of the crossover experience.

The third type of encounter involves us with other dimensions of experience. Effects created by light, sound, spatial dimensions and other sensory appeal can lead meal participants into new levels of experience. Including such effects in the setting for a meal invites psychological expansion and is also a vital part of the crossover experience.

In uniting these three disparate encounters into harmonious dining experiences, we will take as our starting point the food and dining habits of Japan, which themselves have been formed during centuries of influences both native and foreign.

HISTORY OF TABLEWARE

In examining cultural patterns of food and dining, it is essential to maintain a historical perspective. For example, there is undoubtedly a close connection between the development of cities and the development of cultural patterns of dining. The rise of cities and increased travel influence availability of new tableware and foods, which in time transform patterns of eating overall. When this happens, a new cross-cultural style inevitably arises. This process is evident throughout history, the world round.

During the Renaissance, in the 14th–16th centuries, European dining habits underwent significant change as free cities sprang up in Italy and elsewhere, transportation facilities improved, and urban life became more sophisticated. Merchants, scholars, and soldiers took to traveling again after a centuries-long hiatus following the fall of Rome. Trade between Europe and Asia flourished, and by the 16th–17th centuries, utensils from the Far East were having a significant influence on those of the West.

The history of tableware developed along two different paths, separated by India. In countries to the west of India, use of pottery became uppermost, and wares were highly valued for their decorativeness. Palaces of Western nobility contained a "Room for Ceramics," where such wares covered the walls. Thus ceramic wares were valuable as a means of interior decoration.

Westerners first came into contact with Oriental porcelain

after the founding of the British East India Trading Company in 1600, and the Dutch East India Trading Company in 1602. Conveyed to the West on trading ships along with spices, silver, jewels, medicinal herbs, tea and the like, Oriental porcelain created a sensation. Stories survive that porcelain first came to Westerners' attention through shards used as weights in the hold when packing lightweight cargoes such as spices and herbs, and through porcelain tea canisters.

Specifically, Chinese porcelain came to attention in the West at the beginning of the 17th century; the 1620s saw a "chinoiserie boom." In turn, a steady influx of Imari ware in the 1630s provoked a "japonoiserie boom."

These Oriental porcelain wares inspired the production of such famous Western brands of porcelain as Meissen and Limoges. Oriental names such as "Old Imari" continue to survive among Western brand names of porcelain, even now.

Just as Limoges porcelain flourished under the patronage of Madame de Pompadour in 18th century France, development of Western wares has been traditionally connected to patronage by a wealthy aristocratic or merchant class.

In the latter half of the 18th century, the French Revolution brought an end to the aristocratic culture and gave rise in its place to a new culture of the common people, with correspondingly dramatic changes in people's dining habits. Through development of improved manufacturing techniques, people were able to use stoneware instead of wood, metal, and earthenware in their daily lives. The major division in tableware between decorative style, with roots in the aristocratic culture, and functional style, with roots in the later democratic culture, continues today.

Despite some discrepancies in dates, the same general tend-

Namban *("Southern Barbarian") screen; detail*

encies can be traced in Japanese history as well. The earliest known eating utensils date from the first and second centuries B.C. Beginning with glass and pottery, they gradually developed until by the sixth century, the age of envoys to the continent, travel became common and the stimulation of continental exchanges led to rapid sophistication in dining habits.

In the 17th century, the production of porcelain was introduced into Japan from China and Korea, and eating utensils again made a dramatic leap in sophistication. Korean craftsman Yi Sampai came to Japan and opened a kiln at Arita in 1650, producing porcelain for both the feudal aristocracy and wealthy merchant class.

In the beginning Japanese ceramics strongly reflected foreign influences, like many other Japanese crafts. But Japanese craftsmen learned quickly to produce porcelain as high in quality as that from China or Korea. Soon the East India Trading Company were ordering decorative big platters and vessels from Arita and Imari. Townsmen and merchants came into power, and created their own lively culture based on a strong economy. People began using ceramic ware on an everyday basis in place of wood or lacquerware. This age corresponds to that of the Western Renaissance, with many points of similarity in its social background. During this time cultural patterns related to food and dining, especially concerning serving utensils, quickly attained a high level of development.

In the 20th century, and on toward the 21st, the continued diversification and enrichment of eating styles has proven to be a worldwide phenomenon embracing East and West.

Greater awareness of ecology, and of the need for environmental protection and conservation, have been paralleled by increased interest in the problems and potentials of major cities, as the world moves closer together. Today when economic influences prevail, transportation and information networks have become even more highly developed, and people travel more than ever before. In such a fast-paced, stimulating, and responsive world, we can expect cultural patterns related to food and dining to reach new peaks of international sophistication.

It is a challenge, and in my opinion a much-felt need, to meet this milieu with adaptable dining environments which allow participants to fully experience the pleasures of sharing cosmopolitan food and drink. Through creative application of crossover techniques, I believe such dining environments may be achieved.

CHAPTER 1

CROSSOVER TABLESETTINGS

EXPANDING SPACE
IN A NARROW ROOM

A traditional Japanese tea room is the setting for a modern evening of cherry blossom viewing.

A *chashitsu* (Japanese tea room) is narrow by any standard, and by Western standards this space is extraordinarily cramped. Perhaps as a consequence, Japanese have developed a peculiar sense of "expanding space": that is, a limited area that yet allows the heart and mind to expand. Within the confines of a tea room, we sense the limitless expanse of the universe, an experience resembling meditation. The serenity of mind this brings is a distinctive part of Japanese tradition.

To create the impression of expanding space, I made use of traditional Japanese lighting effects. First, the outer garden leading up to the tea room was illuminated by placing lighted candles beside the stone washbasin and elsewhere. Within the tea room the lighting was kept as low as possible; illumination from a low angle accentuates the silhouettes of the utensils, and brings out the soft glow of lacquer bowls.

Western utensils and accessories within this light are informally and unobtrusively arranged; the appearance of Western dishes and utensils, glassware, and Italian candlesticks arranged on the *tatami* alongside Japanese utensils creates a modern sense of harmony (*wa*).

Slide open the paper doors and gaze out on the blooming cherry trees by night; the nearby utensils display a cherry blossom pattern. Inside the tea room, where light and shadow intermingle, the outer world is reflected within the utensils. Such a setting gives full play to the fragility that lies at the heart of the Japanese concept of beauty.

A MODERN ART DECO TABLE

Adding Japanese touches to the Art Deco style provides a sense of freshness and modernity. As this setting shows, traditional Japanese style and Art Deco blend quite harmoniously.

My focus here was on linear beauty, luster, and coolness. The characteristic linear beauty of the Art Deco style derives not simply from clean, straight lines, but also from curves and symmetry, and each of these elements has its corresponding place in traditional Japanese decoration as well. A symmetrical arrangement of lacquer trays and Japanese utensils like this goes particularly well with Art Deco design.

To achieve a soft, elegant luster, silver Art Deco trays and napkin rings were used, along with Art Deco glassware by Lalique, black lacquer trays, and glass chopstick rests. A characteristically monochrome Art Deco color scheme brings out a sense of coolness. The napkins are black, and the flowers arranged in soup glasses are white and green, for a cool and refreshing overall effect.

For the centerpiece, a glasswork representation of Manhattan skyscrapers has been chosen—a most effective sculpture, giving abstract, symbolic expression to the presentation's theme.

EUROPEAN DINING WITH ORIENTAL ACCENTS

This beautifully wallpapered, European-style interior is the inspiration for a tablesetting combining traditional elements with a touch of the exotic. The Laura Ashley wallpaper uses a dark, muted red similar to the Oriental shade known as Cathay red, chosen here as the focus of a color-coordinated setting. Trays, lacquer bowls, chopsticks, and other Japanese utensils on the table are also in Cathay red, with silver candlesticks and cutlery. The floral centerpiece blends in red flowers of a lighter shade. To complement the subdued tone of Cathay red, I placed various other muted Oriental colors on the table, such as the traditional Japanese colors known as the "48 browns and 100 grays," each a distinctive yet subdued tone. Here the sober beige of the tablecloth and the crepe wrappers (*kofukusa*) on the plates set off the dominant red.

The centerpiece was inspired by Dutch still-life paintings of the sixteenth and seventeenth centuries. This is a typically European style of flower arrangement, using lots of fruit and large-petaled flowers. Along with roses, ivy, and grapes, some Oriental accents in the form of peonies, iris leaves, peaches, and plums are included.

WHAT IS CROSSOVER TABLESETTING?

To understand how cultural crossover manifests itself in terms of table presentations, we must consider two basic encounters, the cultural and historical encounters previously mentioned, as our creative launching point. Essentially, crossover blending of traditions is achieved by mixing elements from two or more cultures within the same or different time periods, or one culture during different stages of its development.

While it is true that the world is steadily becoming culturally borderless, we must begin with some cultural foundation if we are to encounter and respond to other cultures. Adopting the standpoint of one particular culture to begin with provides depth and variety to the concept of cultural crossover. So we shall first examine the nature of current attitudes toward food and dining in one specific culture, in this case, Japan.

CHOOSING UTENSILS

The role of table utensils in the crossover experience is fundamental. Let us begin, then, by considering the Japanese experience in this area. Two parallel traditions continue to influence the Japanese outlook on table utensils: one is the epicurean approach, as represented by the contemporary potter Kitaoji Rosanjin (1883–1959), and the other is the *mingei*, or folkcraft, philosophy espoused by Yanagi Soetsu (1889–1961).

Rosanjin's epicurean approach has as its origin Japan's feudal class system. He believed that "eating well is the only criterion for choosing table utensils," and placed prime importance on vessels which should be used to serve only specific kinds of food, or which were indeed made expressly for certain foods. He indulged himself regarding serving dishes, creating many varieties to accompany various foods, and planned the coor-

A classic mingei *bowl by the late master Shoji Hamada*

Bowl in the shape of an abalone shell by Rosanjin

dination between serving vessel and cuisine down to the finest details. A dish suitable for serving carp, for example, would not do for another kind of fish. In addition, just as in the world of kimono, the sense of season was very important; use of different dishes corresponded to changes in the seasons. In cold winter, utensils with a rough, warm texture were to be used; in hot summer, smooth utensils, cool to the touch, were considered appropriate. The relatively large number of serving dishes in the East, and the wide variety of types, are thought to result from this approach.

The *mingei* outlook of Yanagi Soetsu, on the other hand, is based on a philosophy that calls for informal selection of dishes, with its origin in the democratic spirit. Its motto is that "function in daily life provides the basis of decorative art." As long as the vessel remains faithful to its original purpose, its form will automatically be beautiful. For Yanagi, it was important that dishes be suitable to serve a variety of foods.

These two seemingly contradictory ways of thinking about table utensils are each indispensable to the present culture of food and dining in Japan. The epicurean approach expresses a Japanese esthetic sensibility; the *mingei* approach expresses a Japanese philosophy of utilitarianism.

Generally speaking, utensils throughout the world's cultures belong either to an imperial culture (conservative, decorative, traditional), a townsman's culture (contemporary, simple, modern), or an agrarian culture (informal, natural, rustic). In every age, the imperial culture seeks graceful elegance, while the energetic townsman's culture turns against the purely decorative element in art, seeking always simplicity and modernity. The agrarian culture, finally, is always permeated by a timeless and changeless aesthetic. In Japan, Rosan-

jin may be considered in some ways to symbolize the townspeople's culture, Yanagi the agrarian culture.

In planning crossover tablesettings accented by traditional Japanese culture, it is best to combine elements from both the epicurean culture and the folkcraft philosophy to the extent possible.

TEMPORAL ELEMENTS

Crossover tablesettings can be based not only on function and social context, but on more abstract concepts. In addition to their physical manifestations, such as materials and form, utensils each have their own innate personality. In general, they fall into three distinct types:

(1) Utensils that go beyond time. Utensils with artistic appeal or highly individual design, created outside the realm of tradition, are fresh in every age. Plates by Picasso or Cocteau, for example, are eternally new.

(2) Utensils nurtured through time. Conventional utensils nurtured in a long tradition, perfectly suited to their function, fall in this category.

(3) Utensils that belong to a particular time. Included here are trendy utensils, in tune with current fashions; utensils which convey a strong sense of season; and utensils with unusual, playful shapes.

These three types of utensils can be combined in various ways for a particular type of crossover effect. For example: 40% (1), 20% (2), and 40% (3) might be a contemporary crossover. A classic crossover might consist of 20% (1), 60% (2), and 20% (3).

Mixing utensils, in terms of both their physical and abstract characteristics, makes for a more sophisticated, fresh, and striking crossover effect in a tablesetting.

A "VICTORIAN CHINESE" ARRANGEMENT

From the early 20th century to the 1930s, a spirit of cultural crossover spread across China. This era's brilliant blend of Chinese and European elements serves as a basis for a contemporary interpretation of a Chinese-European tablesetting.

European style was the foundation—the concept of a centerpiece (here a soup tureen surrounded by flowers) is clearly European in origin. The plates, glasses, and cutlery, the black-and-white checkerboard floor, and the white lace curtains are all traditionally European in style, and more specifically, Victorian.

To add Chinese elements, I turned first to color. Camel became the main tone, the preferred color of a succession of Chinese emperors; for flowers, napkins, and other focal points a range of colors from camel to orange was used.

For additional decoration, a set of T'ang three-color glazed horse figurines, in a variety of poses, lends a graceful suggestion of the ancient Silk Road.

Next I turned my attention to the utensils, choosing from among the creations of Richard Ginori those most Oriental in color and design. Details such as these blend in with the overall European style, to produce a natural eclecticism that might be labeled "Victorian Chinese."

EXAMPLES OF CROSSOVER DINING PRESENTATIONS

Japanese and Western crossover in a decorative and formal style

When combining Japanese and Western styles, a natural harmony can be achieved by using the conservative and decorative imperial culture as a basis, providing an image of *japonoiserie*, but complemented by Western accessories. The goal should be an epicurean feast. The Japanese contribution might be, for example, decorative lacquerware. Combined with an equivalent level of Western formal tableware, a magnificent harmony can be achieved.

When combining Japanese and Indian, Thai, or other Oriental styles, however, wares in the folkcraft style fit more easily. Oriental wares with a strongly informal and natural look are representative of agrarian cultures. Appropriate Japanese accessories include Bizen ware and handcrafted paper. Such items of rough, warm simplicity blend in with other informal wares in perfect naturalness.

When mixing Western and Chinese styles, the townsman culture approach works best, conveying a more contemporary, urban image. To introduce a note of sophistication, use focal points, such as a thin silk cloth set casually on the tabletop.

Contrasting materials of lacquer, handcrafted paper, and bone china

Silk crepe furoshiki *using tones from the Japanese "48 browns and 100 grays"*

A rustic setting incorporates the folkcraft style

HOW TO CONVEY
A SENSE OF JAPANESE AMBIENCE

Here are several points to remember when constructing a crossover tablesetting to convey a sense of Japanese ambience.

First, remember to combine contrasting materials. Silk crepe and stainless steel, bamboo and glass, porcelain and pottery, crystal and lacquerware, stone and paper: the use of such contrasting materials evokes a Japanese mood. In the West, it is standard to stick to a single material and style of presentation in a formal setting, but in Japan the use of differing materials is appreciated.

Second, use distinctively Japanese colors. Japan has a traditional set of colors known as the "48 browns and 100 grays", all marked by a subdued, grayish tone. If colors of this type are used in the tablesetting, a Japanese atmosphere can be obtained.

Keep the setting low off the floor. In the West, ceiling height is a measure of beauty, but in Japan a low, wide setting is the ideal. The use of straight lines and squares, as in *shoji* and *tatami* (paper screens and straw mats), is another distinctive feature of Japanese interior decoration.

Break up symmetrical arrangements.

In the West the beauty of symmetry is stressed, but in Japan, asymmetry is prized. Using an asymmetrical arrangement of Western-style utensils is an effective way to gain a crossover effect.

Make the most of tactile impressions: smooth surfaces such as those of lacquerware and stainless steel; rough surfaces, as in Bizen and Shigaraki wares; natural, aromatic surfaces as in cedarwood and green bamboo. By using materials such as these, with their strong appeal to the senses, especially the sense of touch, a Japanese tone can be easily achieved.

Add something traditional from the tablesetting theme's country or region, in this case Japan, such as an antique lacquer utensil. This technique of adding a traditional utensil can be used to create other crossover ambience. For Chinese ambience, try something with a dragon motif; for Balinese ambience, a folk object with a bird motif. Use traditional handicrafts of whatever country's ambience is serving as the basis for the setting.

Finally, use light. For a Japanese mood, light should be low and oblique, not direct. This alone is enough to evoke a Japanese atmosphere.

A tactile statement is made with stainless steel and iron

CHAPTER 2

TABLESETTING THROUGH THE SEASONS

A
CHERRY BLOSSOM
PARTY
IN A MODERN
SETTING

In the Heian period (794–1185), courtiers enjoyed the elegant spring pastime of composing poems beneath the cherry blossoms; that graceful and refined mood is recreated here in a modern arrangement on wooden floor.

Cherry blossom viewing provides an occasion to relax under a cherry tree massed with blossoms, and drink your fill of their beauty. In order to come as close to this ideal as possible, small portable platforms were used on top of regular wooden flooring to give the feeling of *tatami* (straw matting). The platforms are 90 centimeters (about three feet) square and 20 centimeters (about eight inches) high. Several of them were combined, laying cushions and utensils on top.

On either side, large boughs of flowering cherry were placed, to create the illusion of being surrounded by cherry trees indoors. There is a basic color scheme of pink, white, and black to match the colors of blossoms and branches. Pink plates sit atop black lacquer trays, alongside Western dishes with a cherry blossom motif. Shocking pink napkins accent the setting, while frosted beverage glasses suggest a hazy curtain of flowers.

Beneath the cherry boughs, pale pink rosé champagne makes a pleasant drink. In place of trays, strips of *tanzaku*—fancy paper used for writing poems—carry traditional spring confections. Food and drink alike thus convey a touch of springtime.

AN OUTDOOR PARTY
WITH KOREAN ACCENTS

Not all picnics need be casual; from time to time it is pleasant to aim for a more elegant outing reminiscent of the pastimes of the old aristocracy. For a picnic with china, glassware, and cutlery that yet manages to blend easily with nature, an ethnic touch is helpful.

A Korean-style presentation can be particularly effective. First, for a lunchbox containing all the picnic food and supplies, a Korean mahogany chest originally designed to hold clothing has been select-ed. For a picnic table, a tennis-court bench does nicely. On it, china, cutlery, and glasses from Tiffany for each person are set out, along with Korean metal bowls and chopsticks. Bunches of wildflowers give just the right finishing touch.

The secret of successfully blending such disparate elements lies in the skillful use of color. The base color here is bright pink, a traditional Korean color. The same color appears in the chinaware and flowers, set off stylishly by deep navy lunchmats.

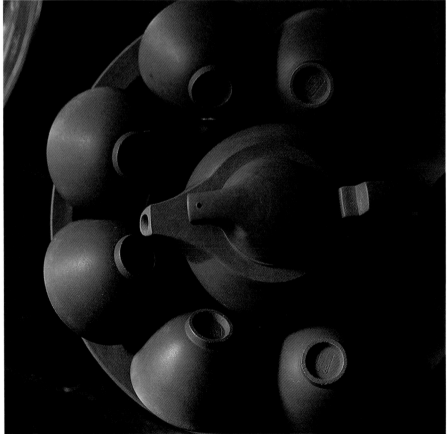

AN ORIENTAL
TEA PARTY

For a tea party with tea and sweets, one wants the atmosphere of a salon, where conversation can freely swirl. Here Cathay red is the base color, with an assortment of tea items of East and West to serve as conversation pieces. On the silver tray is a Chinese tea service, surrounded by Japanese *fukusa* (decorative silk crepe squares). Western utensils are in general smooth to the touch, so the rough feel of Oriental fabric and pottery gives a strong flavor of the Far East. The smooth silver tray, combined with the roughness of the tea pourer and silk squares, will delight guests. Conversation pieces are scattered throughout the room, from the traditional Russian samovar to the antique Chinese screen, the unusual flower arrangement, and the traditional Japanese "beckoning cat." Creating a melange of items designed to provoke conversation is another way to evoke the spirit of crossover.

A cherry blossom arrangement

Color coordination using tanzaku *paper and pastel-colored confectionery*

ON SPRING

THE ESSENCE OF SPRING

In Japanese society, the spring months of March and April traditionally mark the end of one year and the start of another. Spring is a season of joyous renewal. The Japanese celebration of spring is comparable to the Western custom of dressing up in new clothes for Easter, and spring tablesettings should reflect a similar change of apparel. The Japanese have a charming custom of combining utensils of green bamboo and glassware only after spring has fully arrived.

For ways to enjoy the seasons, nothing provides clearer guidance than the world of Japanese tea ceremony. Tea master Sen no Rikyu (1522–1591) set forth three important points regarding the observance of spring in the tea ceremony. One is to strive for taste or elegance, devising special ways to present spring through the appropriate utensils, accessories, and colors. It is a sign of discriminating taste to suggest spring indirectly through the judicious use of pale pink, for example, rather than by automatically trotting out a design of cherry blossoms. Another is to make the most of the blessings of nature. Lighting is an effective way to evoke spring, and warm sunshine in particular goes well in this season. It is important to incorporate natural sunlight skillfully, taking advantage of light streaming through cherry branches of windows. Finally, the presentation should be characterized by *magokoro*, or thoughtful sincerity. Having cocktail preparations and appetizers all set out, burning subtle incense or playing background music help to make guests feel that their arrival has been fully anticipated. Such similar thoughtful touches make a lasting impression.

Playing with box containers and delicate confectionery shapes

Lacquerware reflecting spring's soft lighting

AN ELEGANT LUNCH AT THE RIVERSIDE

By a window overlooking the waterfront, diners can enjoy their meal while bathed in soft sunshine. A perky table decor based on an elegant shade of green is the perfect setting for a spring lunch.

First, notice the Biedermeier-style interior. This decor originated in early nineteenth-century Vienna, and its sophisticated use of straight lines bears much similarity to the geometric beauty of traditional Japanese design. The green lines of the window frame are most distinctive, and I have tried to echo them in the table setting. Around the table the primary color is green, set off by black and ivory. The napkins are green, and the tablecloth is ivory silk crepe bordered in black. The chairs are of unpainted wood.

The flower arrangement is contained in a traditional square green lacquer box. The flowers are callas, a favorite in Biedermeier style. The beauty of imbalance is part of traditional Japanese aesthetics; an asymmetrical arrangement evokes the feeling of flowers spilling from an open container.

Arranging Western cuisine in the formal *kaiseki* style of Japan is another effective way to enjoy a sense of crossover between two worlds.

Lustrous lacquerware

Silk crepe napkins

HOW TO PLAN SPRING PRESENTATIONS

(1) Colors

Use pale tints. In the traditional scheme of Japanese colors, this means *kasane-iro* or "layered colors," the paler hues used in kimonos. Light tones such as these are most suitable for spring. In choosing a shade of green, for example, the pale green of new grass is most desirable.

(2) Nature and Spring Light

Use flowers. Spring is the season of flowers in general, and of cherry blossoms in particular in Japan. A setting, whether indoors or outdoors, that illuminates nature also conveys a springlike quality. Enhance the beauty of the light with a glossy tablecloth, lacquered utensils, or other materials with reflecting surfaces. For an indoor setting, to convey a Japanese sense of spring, artificial light should come from a low and oblique angle.

(3) Thoughtful Touches

One way to increase the joy of freedom from the long winter is through the invigorating pleasure of new encounters. A spring outing is the ideal occasion. In the West, a picnic is a pastoral amusement, full of rustic charm, but in Japan gathering for a meal outdoors has been traditionally considered an extremely elegant and refined leisure activity. Human encounters and pleasant interaction with nature were regarded as the highest form of recreation. One way to share in the spirit of such outdoor gatherings nowadays is to take special pains with the seating arrangement. The surprise and pleasure of meeting new people and renewing old acquaintances will add to the joy of spring's arrival.

SPRING UTENSILS

The most characteristic feature of tableware for spring is medium thickness, in transition from the heaviness of winter tableware to the thinness of summer ones. Examples are old Kiyomizu, Kurita, and other porcelain wares with fine surface cracks.

Lustrous utensils, such as lacquerware, pair well with spring sunshine. Red lacquer is more suitable than black to express the joyousness of spring.

Heavy pottery, as well as tablecloths and napkins made of silk crepe, also have a rough texture that evokes the warmth of springtime.

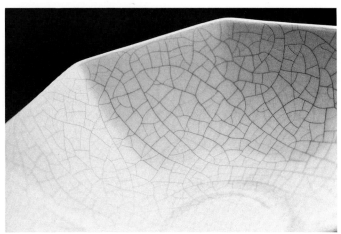

Porcelain featuring fine surface cracks

An example of delicate Mishima ware

A CANDLE-LIT POOLSIDE PARTY

For a poolside party on a summer's evening, I sought to create a mood of solemn elegance. Water, light, and bamboo are the elements contributing to a sense of East-West crossover.

Acrylic boxes were lined up alongside the pool to suggest *hakozen*, boxes used in formal Japanese meals. A glass and a pair of chopsticks were placed within each stacked box, and arranged on top of each plate were a black lacquer bowl and napkin. At poolside it is only common sense to use unbreakable materials, but that is no reason to trot out paper cups and paper plates every time. The slight tension created by combining lacquerware, china, and glassware contributes to a mood of special elegance on such an occasion.

A poolside setting offers unique opportunities for flowers and lighting. "Flower rafts," floating arrangements of flowers on green bamboo and a traditional method of enjoying flowers in Japan, take on special appeal at poolside. For illumination I lined up candles alongside the pool, floating them on bamboo rafts. The reflected glow and the bobbing of the flames add a mysterious beauty.

To evoke a sense of coolness, a monochromatic color scheme works best, accented here by the bright yellow of flowers and plates.

A PARTY
IN A LOFT

How about having a party in a loft that serves as an artist's studio? When assembling people in a space decorated with dynamic paintings on the walls, for balance the table coordination should be as simple as possible. The eating space should harmonize easily with the paintings, allowing them to play the dominant role.

Here I focused on the monochrome borders of the paintings, choosing inconspicuous, neutral colors for flowers and cuisine alike, and arranging them in a simple symmetrical design. On the table were placed small antique trays known as *nanasun kozen*, decorated with bits of *amuses-gueules*. Using utensils all of the same design is the basis of table coordination in the West; using antique Oriental utensils for the purpose creates fresh interest.

Moreover the beauty of empty space on the table echoes the spatial composition of the paintings. Apart from the trays nothing else was set out, not even glassware or chopsticks. The chairs at either end of the table hold tiered picnic boxes containing the main dish. Lofts generally have a bar counter or comparable space set off in a corner, which I took advantage of to set out drinks, chopsticks, cutlery, and napkins away from the table, in a simple buffet style.

A SUMMER LUNCH IN A JAPANESE-STYLE ROOM

Here is a fresh setting for an early summer lunch, with blue as the color theme. The runner on the table is powder blue, and the dishes are basically blue and white. Placing a large number of glasses on the table creates a cool atmosphere. Pale blue flowers were chosen for the centerpiece to match the dishes and stemware.

In detail, the soupcups and saucers are of the Blue Onion series made in Meissen in the eighteenth century; the large plates are Royal Copenhagen, by an artist active in the Art Nouveau period; the gourd-shaped dishes on them are traditional Japanese blue-and-white porcelain; the cutlery is of Art Deco design; the stemware is an assortment, for drinks from champagne to liqueur.

This setting, which gathers together utensils of various periods and nationalities, was inspired by the Japanese ideal of tea ceremony for literati. The scholars and poets of Japan in bygone days would amuse themselves at tea gatherings by bringing out utensils of diverse ages and discussing them. This setting offers the chance for an even more subtle and graceful entertainment, through the free mixing of items from different places as well as different times.

A SUMMERTIME TABLE WITH ACRYLIC AND BAMBOO

Over many years, the Japanese have developed a particular style for summertime meals. To begin with, eating utensils are made of bamboo, particularly green bamboo. Effective use is made of water as an accessory, and fresh greenery is set out for the Japanese dinner table. Such innovations, helped create a mood of elegant coolness for the table.

A Western tablesetting incorporating such Japanese seasonal touches is an appealing example of crossover coordination.

First, I set out transparent acrylic vases in the center of the table, filled them with water, and arranged flowers on floating plates of green bamboo. I used green bamboo and acrylic at each place setting as well, placing an acrylic board over two runners of green bamboo, and arranging the place setting on top. Cut-glass tumblers, glass dishes, green leaves, and other items convey a sense of coolness.

The central theme is one of floating: the bamboo floats on water, the acrylic trays set on green bamboo seem to float in air. Together all these elements suggest the gentle motion of a summer breeze. The final touch—typically Western-style floral tablecloth—gives the entire arrangement added freshness and novelty.

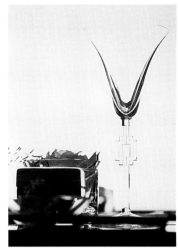

The cool clarity of Lalique.

An ethnic-style arrangement brings out spatial dimensions

ON SUMMER

THE ESSENCE OF SUMMER

My interpretation of a summer ambience is drawn from the esthetics of the Japanese tea ceremony and Western ideas, resulting in a contemporary approach incorporating ethnic touches. I sought not only to project a sense of tranquil coolness, but also to suggest the power and energy representative of summer.

In his writings, tea master Sen no Rikyu lists three conditions necessary to convey a sense of summer. One of them is the "scattering of dew," which relates to anything suggesting the coolness or transparency of water, such as water sprinkled on the ground or pouring into a stone washbasin. Placing a water-filled basin on the table or using the water of a pool in the background are other ways to achieve this.

Rikyu's next instruction is to entertain with a "light taste." Adding this lightness in taste to the basic flavors—sweet, salty, sour, bitter, and pungent—is especially suited to summertime meals.

Finally, it is important to achieve a sense of "coolness." A summer tea ceremony features reed screens and mats, glassware, fragrant cedar boards, etc. In the West, a summery setting could include such light and airy elements as lace, glassware, sunlight filtering through leaves, etc.

A dramatic use of water

AN EXOTIC
ETHNIC DINNER

The sense in which the word "ethnic" is used here calls for a grand stretch of the imagination, sweeping back through time to ancient civilizations.

To capture this sense of ethnicity, it is necessary to use natural materials. On the floor is a straw mat, and hanging from the ceiling is a curtain made of handcrafted paper (*washi*), while many of the serving dishes are of marble. The materials were scrupulously selected to emphasize tactile qualities: the coolness of Thai silk cushions; the roughness of terra-cotta vases; the smoothness of polished marble. Participants should enjoy nature with all their senses. The color scheme was organized around stone and earth tones, with gradations from beige to brown. The contrast of light and shadow was also carefully orchestrated, with indirect lighting lending a sense of depth to spatial surroundings.

A balanced design helps to create mood of solemn dignity. In the vase at center rear is a symmetrical arrangement of Egyptian papyrus, which together with the mounds of fruits and confections creates a sacred atmosphere, like that of an ancient temple.

Thai silk and handcrafted paper, ceramics and terra cotta—the harmonious beauty created from such surprising combinations also projects an exquisite exoticism.

HOW TO PLAN SUMMER PRESENTATIONS

(1) Water

It is essential to incorporate water somehow into the setting, perhaps by locating a party in a poolside garden, or setting an acrylic or glass bowl full of water on the table. Earthenware, cedar boards, green bamboo and the like should all be dipped in water before setting them on the table. Using water in this way not only suggests coolness to the eye, but also—in the case of cedar and bamboo—releases subtle natural fragrances which deepen the impression of summer.

(2) Natural Sound

The ripple of flowing water. The tinkle of wind-chimes. The rustle of leaves in a breeze. Incorporating such natural sounds can greatly enhance the suggestion of coolness.

(3) Tactile Impressions

Chilled marble. The soft dryness of straw mats. The pleasing roughness of Thai silk, textiles, and handcrafted paper (*washi*). Props like these, which appeal directly to the senses, should be used in an informal manner.

(4) Shadows

Use light filtered through a reed or paper screen, or through flowers and plants. To suggest coolness, begin with the pleasing gradations between light and shadow.

Evoking summer through the transparency of glass

Blue and white porcelain is perfect for summer settings

SUMMER UTENSILS

No material creates the effect of coolness like glassware. Long ago in Japan, glass, introduced from the West, was extremely rare and expensive. The custom of reserving precious glassware for the brief summer season has left an indelible association in the Japanese mind between glassware and the joys of summer.

High-tech materials such as acrylic, stainless steel, and a sheet of glass are also handy. By reflecting light or background scenery from their surfaces, such materials express coolness in a contemporary style.

Decorating the tabletop with various dark stones and rough pieces of granite moistened with water can also make a summer gathering more refreshing and enjoyable.

Blue and white porcelain is ideal for summer, the color combination conveys coolness. Use various shades of blue to enhance this effect.

Green bamboo sprinkled with water

Marble's cool image brings out the beauty of natural materials

Acrylic is paired with greenery for a refreshing effect

AN ART-APPRECIATION DINNER

One of the special rituals that takes place in the Japanese tea room is the "viewing of the hanging scroll." At the beginning of the tea ceremony, the scroll is brought in a box and then taken out and hung in the *tokonoma*, or alcove, for guests to gaze on and enjoy. Here let us consider ways to transfer this ritual enjoyably to a Western-style space.

For example, a ritual of "hanging an oil painting on the wall" might be incorporated into the beginning of the dinner. Here a loft functions in place of the tea room, and the party begins with the host hanging an oil painting on the main wall. One of the ways in which people of taste in old Japan enhanced the experience of mealtimes was through appreciation of scrolls. By extending that concept, a painting can function as a conversation piece; the painter, style, contents, and mood portrayed are all good sources of lively dinner-table talk.

For the setting, I have tried to suggest the feeling of a tea room in crossover style. I gathered various Japanese items, such as handcrafted paper (*washi*) tablemats, indigo-dyed napkins, chopsticks, and pottery, in a Western-style arrangement. On one corner of the table is a kind of vase used in the tea ceremony, known as *hana byobu* (flower screen), in which I have arranged seasonal flowers. Underglaze blue porcelain plates with traditional Oriental patterns are used to give the table its final look of both crossover and contemporaneity.

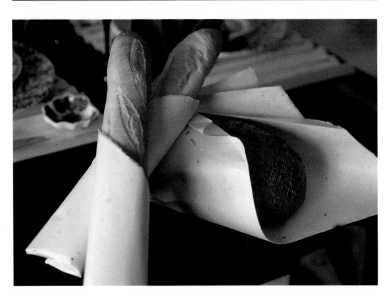

A MOON VIEWING BANQUET

If spring cherry blossom viewing is the epitome of elegance, autumn moon viewing is rather a time to enjoy a spirit of pastoral, rustic pleasure.

To enjoy moon viewing on a Western-style floor, tatami stands are useful. To suggest the mood of autumn, each one is wrapped in russet silk crepe. Lighting suggests the tone of moonlight, while lacquer trays with crescent-shaped handles suggest the shape of the moon.

The dominant color of the setting is reddish-brown. For accent, bright yellow chrysanthemums or orchids do nicely.

Silver and gold bring out the rich glow of autumn colors. The glistening of silver and gold patterns on lacquerware, or of silver and gold thread in floor cushions, will stand out all the more in moonlight.

It is also sometimes fun to adopt motifs from legends associated with the moon.

According to Japanese legend, there is a rabbit on the moon, pounding rice-cakes; to pick up on that theme, rabbit figurines are placed here and there. Instead of sweet round rice dumplings, a traditional moon-viewing snack, try a bowlful of walnuts, or chocolates. Simplicity, warmth, and relaxation are well suited to a modern evening of moon viewing.

A HARVEST PICNIC

For an outdoor party with an enjoyable new twist, I combined a traditional Japanese boxed-lunch outing with a classic Western-style picnic.

First, wheat patterned *kasuri* (ikat print) runners are spread on a carpet of fallen leaves, with wildflowers in the center and cloth-wrapped boxed lunches around the perimeter, in the style of an old-fashioned outing. Beside each boxed lunch are a coffee cup and a small bouquet of flowers, together with a bamboo basket filled with bread, champagne, and champagne glasses, in the mood of a Western outdoor party.

Color provides the focal point. Since the setting is outdoors, vivid colors like the bright red of the cloth wrappers are used to contrast with the more subdued colors of nature.

To enjoy such an outing, it is necessary to plan every detail, and spare no effort. Throughout history, especially in the Orient, the urge to indulge in the simplicities of nature has inspired the imagination. A stack of logs can be a table, with wildflowers the centerpiece; withered branches can provide decoration; a stone can serve as a side-table; and the perfume of trees can impart its fragrance to the whole setting. Take the time to relax, and let your imagination go.

Tea canisters make imaginative holders for nuts, dried fruits, crackers and other accompaniments. Line up the canisters inside a basket and fill them with various nibbles. It's also nice if someone can write the contents of each canister on the lid in calligraphy, using a brush. Use the lids as plates.

A RELAXING BUSINESS LUNCH

At lunchtime between rounds of business, an attractive atmosphere around the table can create a wonderful feeling of relaxation. To arrange such an occasion, I designed a crossover tablesetting using lots of nature and fresh air.

Again, the basic color scheme uses earth colors. Brown, reddish brown, orange—the warm colors of earth, fire, and flowers—are featured in the tablecloth and utensils alike. Materials must be chosen with equal care. Vessels of earthenware and bamboo, cloth of hemp and silk: as much as possible, only natural materials. A terra-cotta soup tureen is set amid desert flowers, which provide a refreshing fragrance in the center of the table. The spoon rest and the bread plates are also pottery. The placemats, from Southeast Asia, are woven bamboo, and the tablecloth is Japanese hemp printed in a lattice design. Whatever their origin, natural materials have an intriguing affinity.

Against the wall at the back of the table, I placed a large arrangement of tropical plants and flowers as the focal point of the setting. It functions rather like the alcove (*tokonoma*) in a traditional Japanese room. The Oriental decorating concept of placing a bold floral arrangement near the seat of honor works forcefully here to integrate this multinational table setting.

An autumn reminder—the warm brown of walnuts

Handcrafted paper with the guest's name is tied to the back of each chair

Grapes symbolize the harvest

ON AUTUMN

THE ESSENCE OF AUTUMN

If spring in Japan is the season for a heart tuned to festive joyousness, as symbolized by cherry blossom viewing, autumn is the season for quiet refinement. Spring is youthful and gay, autumn a time to savor mature pleasures.

Above all, autumn is a time to celebrate the harvest's bounty, so any tablesetting in this season should evoke as much as possible the pleasures of eating. This is true in the West also; for example, celebrating the arrival of Beaujolais Nouveau expresses the joy of the harvest season.

In Japan many traditional annual observances involve the love of nature, especially in autumn, including moon viewing, leaf collecting, harvest festivals, and chrysanthemum festivals, and it can be great fun to choose one of these traditional pursuits as the occasion for a party.

The main point to keep in mind is to emphasize the harvest, and the sense of taste. The menu should include plenty of foods and drinks suggestive of harvest time. Warmth is also a key factor; table utensils and fabrics of warm colors should be chosen to express a spirit of ease and welcome.

A TEATIME SETTING IN
LINES AND CURVES

This teatime setting in a dining room watched over by the portrait of an exotic-looking woman, harmonizes two aesthetic senses, the Chinese and the Japanese.

The first notable element on the table is the combination of colors: beige tablecloth, brown bowls, burnt-orange utensils, bronze flowerstands and napkins. The harmony of earth and metal hues creates a multidimensional beauty of the highest order.

This setting also combines linear and curvilinear beauty. The flowerstands are lined up in a row. The plates are covered with sheets of handcrafted paper (*washi*) on which lacquer bowls are placed, and chopsticks laid at exact right angles to the edge of the paper. Such straight lines, the foundation of Japanese table settings, are enhanced by the exotic curves of Chinese-style table ornaments.

Oriental flowers, rowan blossoms, and amaryllis, are paired with Western ivy. The expression on the face of the woman looking down on this crossover arrangement symbolizes the elegant mood of this afternoon tea.

HOW TO PLAN AUTUMN PRESENTATIONS

(1) Tactile Impressions

Rustic pottery is suitable for the fall. In spring, light-colored, thinner, more feminine pottery such as Hagi ware is called for, whereas in the fall dark-colored, heavy, more masculine-style pottery is ordinarily used. The feel and weight in the hand of such rough-textured pottery conveys a particular warmth. Materials should be pongee, ikat, or something similar which is pleasant to the touch.

(2) Colors

Use warm colors. In particular, bitter-sweet, a rust-red color midway between vermilion and brown, is representative of fall colors. A heavy Shigaraki ware with a pattern brushed on in bitter-sweet gives a distinct feeling of fall. In general, tones from brown to red and yellow should be used effectively in dishes, cloths, and accessories.

(3) Subtle Refinement

Portraying autumn with a subtle, mature flair adds to the refinement and elegance of any gathering at this time of year. For example, in the world of Japanese tea ceremony, autumn is the season of beginning. New tea comes out in November, with special ceremonies to mark the occasion. Held while the fall leaves are at the height of their beauty, these ceremonies are particularly striking. Similar sophisticated gatherings are possible with a Western slant, and are appropriate for autumn presentations.

The uneven weave of pongee gives a natural feeling

The warm tones of autumn in a furoshiki

Tableware that depicts the autumn moon

Roughness of materials conveys the season

Pottery, well-formed and graceful

AUTUMN UTENSILS

The most important qualification for materials to use in autumn is that they convey a sense of warmth. Utensils, for example, should be heavy, rustic, and make a statement, such as Bizen or Shigaraki ware. Utensils of bronze or iron, such as an iron teapot or a bronze vase, also impart an autumnal air. Handcrafted paper (*washi*) can also certainly be used to advantage.

A GOLD AND BLUE CHRISTMAS FOR TWO

The occasion is an opulent Christmas dinner for two in a spacious setting. Candlelight sets the stage for an extravagant, solemn, and dramatic evening.

The focal points of the setting are the Victorian-era tablecloth and the antique Old Imari ware bowls. Both traditions are characterized by their ornate decoration, which are displayed to best advantage in dim light. The theme colors are royal blue and gold. The elements of this setting are highly individualized; the decorative utensils were produced in completely different places and eras, but they blend together with amazing harmony.

To increase the romance and excitement of the occasion, clusters of tall candles decorate the tabletop. They have the same solemn dignity of candles in church, but here they convey the sense of a special Christmas. A Thai bowl, decorated with miniature gold horns, serves well to cool champagne.

The Christmas to be shared here is a fanciful occasion for adults, not in the least childish or sentimental.

A CHRISTMAS DINNER WITH ASIAN ACCENTS

The essential colors for a Christmas setting are red and green. Red suggests Santa Claus, green Christmas trees. Motifs with a Biblical significance are included here: birds, since they are the emissaries of the Holy Spirit; withered branches, to suggest the stable and the crown of thorns; candles, to light people's feet; and aromatic substances, to suggest the gifts of the Magi to the Christ child.

The tablecloth is a silk crepe cloth of deep green. In the center is a Japanese version of a Christmas tree, consisting of a stack of ten red lacquer boxes, tied with a green ribbon and topped with a corsage of pine boughs, pine cones, and holly.

The dishes at each placesetting are a blend of East and West, consisting of a large green Western plate with gold rims, topped with a medium-sized plate of Old Imari ware; a red napkin with a wreath design; bird ornaments from Bali; Korean spoons; and small dishes of Old Imari for bread and butter.

Pine boughs, cones, aromatic tea leaves, and spice cookies fill an antique Old Imari bowl. In the background, a gold screen is fenced in by two Christmas trees. The bowl rests on branches of holly, fir, and fragrant lilies. All of these elements merge to create an eclectic Christmas evening that is at once sacred and festive.

AN OFFICE COCKTAIL PARTY

The secret of a successful after-hours office cocktail party lies in carrying it off effortlessly, with minimal expenditure of time and trouble.

The object of this table setting was to demonstrate how swiftly an office space can be transformed from its daytime image. First, all the office lights were switched off, leaving only the glow of candles. Simply wrapping sheets of hand-crafted paper (*washi*) around the candle-stands lends added drama.

In choosing utensils and cloth, the objective should be to convey a feeling of warmth, since normally offices abound in cold materials like stainless steel, acrylic,

and plastic. I selected wood and earthen-ware utensils, with napkins, cloth, and runner of *kasuri* (splashed pattern) and *tsumugi* (pongee) cotton prints. This in itself goes far towards softening the sharp-ness of the office interior.

Square lacquer trays are arranged in a checkered pattern against a window; on them are set earthenware saké cups and plates, lacquer bowls and chopsticks, splash-dyed napkins, and other Japanese-style items. At either end of the table are tiered boxes containing food, and candle-stands wrapped in paper. One corner of the impersonal office now contains an inviting, warm Japanese-style buffet.

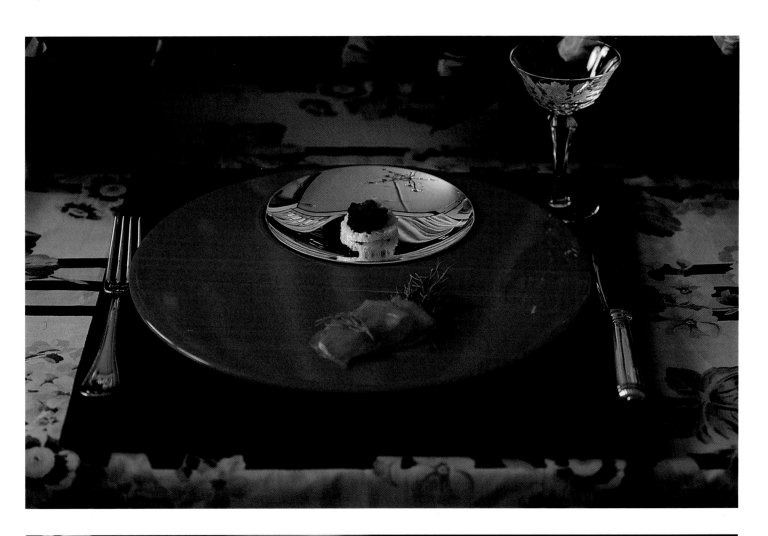

A COSMOPOLITAN
NEW YEAR'S PARTY

A Japanese New Year's celebration is a formal holiday, accented here with touches of European utensils and decorations.

A British cloth of modern design was chosen for the tablecloth, a twentieth-century adaptation of a popular Victorian pattern combining flowers and black ribbon. The main color is black, accented by vermilion and yellow. On the table are individual square trays covered with black silk crepe, surmounted with round plates of yellowish-red lacquer.

Japanese eating utensils divide naturally into three traditional categories: *shin, gyo*, and *so*. An occasion such as New Year's calls for utensils of the formal, *shin* style. In lacquerware, this translates into bright vermilion dishes of perfectly round or square shape. This setting combines square trays, round red lacquer plates, and silver, a formal material in the European tradition.

In the center of the table are a black lacquer vase with yellow roses, a black Wedgwood bowl, and a Meissen clown figurine; the chandelier overhead adds to the beauty of this eclectic presentation.

ON WINTER

THE ESSENCE OF WINTER

Winter has many facets. It can be a time to reflect, and to wind up the year's affairs. It can also be a time of frenzied activity in preparation for year-end and New Year festivities. The joys of the outdoors also beckon, creating many opportunities for enjoyable gatherings.

In Japanese tradition, New Year's itself corresponds to the start of spring. Winter is symbolized by year-end events, many of which are filled with a sense of anticipation of the coming year. The end of the year marks the change in the traditional zodiac cycle, and this can be reflected in tablesettings. If, for example, the year is changing from the Year of the Boar to the Year of the Mouse, the table can feature appropriate figurines, such as that of a boar facing backwards.

However winter is interpreted, a seasonal table presentation should include two main elements. One is the sense of warmth, best expressed by the presence of fire (or firelike energy). This might be a dining space with a cozy, brightly-lit fireplace. Or it might be a hot, steaming cauldron of delectables, cooking right at the dining table, inviting family and friends to gather around for a comforting meal.

The other element a winter presentation should include is a touch of the beauty and drama of winter—the magic of a snowy landscape, the serene beauty of untouched snow, the invigorating cold, the star-studded night sky, the excitement of a day of winter sports. Bringing in this element can be done in ingenious and pleasurable ways.

Candles harmonizing with nature

Against a backdrop of snow, a single rose makes a dramatic statement

A playful evocation of winter

A DRAMATIC EVENING IN AN ITALIAN MOOD

Sipping fine saké while apprecia-
tively at a snowy scene is a time-
honored winter tradition in Japan. I've
taken this custom and freely altered it for
a Western setting, while still retaining the
spirit of enjoying snow.

Italy is the theme of the evening, with
the world of opera as an extra added
dimension.

An Italian-style space is created that
uses the colors of the Italian flag—red,
green, and white. Japanese elements are
added on the table in the form of lacquerware and chopsticks. Nested boxes are
filled with snow and topped with a silver
tray bearing antipasto, while lacquer
bowls are filled with spinach ravioli for a
striking crossover effect.

The interplay of candlelight and the
shine of lacquer creates a sense of quiet
anticipation, tying in with the dramatic
mood of opera before the curtains go up.

Evoking the mood of snow-viewing
calls for a sense of playfulness above all:
spangles sprinkled on the table, red roses
festooning vases. To light the footpath by
the entrance, snow-packed lacquer utensils have been set out, each holding a
candle and a red rose.

A heavy, solid Bizen saké container

HOW TO PLAN WINTER PRESENTATIONS

(1) Fire
Gathering around the table for a hearty meal, with cooking done right at the table, conveys warmth directly by the presence of fire.

(2) Folkcrafts
Choose fabrics with a strongly rustic image, such as pongee or *sashiko* (white decorative stitching on indigo-dyed blue cloth). Western quilting also conveys the warmth of craftsmanship, mixing casually with tableware and cutlery.

(3) Sense of Sharing
Adding a homelike touch to the gaiety of Christmas conveys a sense of warmth. For example, instead of a tree as a table centerpiece, place the main dish in nested boxes of green lacquer, stacking them up on the table from the largest to the smallest to look like a tree. Sharing the contents of the boxes is an excellent way to experience the joys of love and friendship.

(4) Awareness of Winter
Bringing a sense of winter into an indoor setting through symbolic or visual means can result in a pleasing seasonal presentation. Play up the beauty of the season by filling a container with snow to cool a bottle of wine, or pile snow in a table utensil as a decoration, or make a tablesetting that incorporates straw suggestive of a shelter from snow.

Nested lacquer boxes help in sharing the loving spirit of the season

A large, lacquered Goroku bowl

WINTER UTENSILS

Earthenware pots, saké or wine-bottle containers and the like should be heavy and solid, with deep colors. Hagi ware and Shigaraki ware are excellent examples; choose large items with a sense of weight. Among porcelain, Ki-seto ware; among stoneware, Tokoname, Mashiko, Bankoyaki, and Bizen wares are good. Large bowls, large plates, and large saké holders are especially effective in wintertime.

Fabrics of dark blue and red also help to create a feeling of keeping the winter cold at bay. Rough fabrics have special appeal. Heavy fabrics have been used in Japan for centuries to wrap the rice tub for insulation.

Lacquerware especially suitable for winter includes Goroku-wan and Negoro-nuri, wares that are very large and rough in design. Wooden utensils of rough and dynamic design are also suitable for winter.

Cooking at the table conveys a feeling of warmth

A large serving platter presents a variety of tastes

Ikat (kasuri) fabrics have an exotic appeal

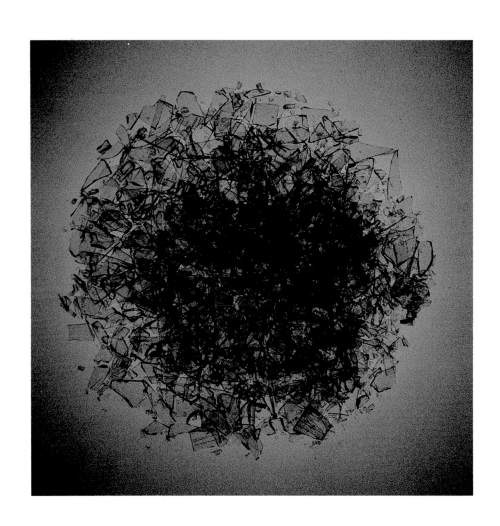

CHAPTER 3
TABLESETTING

Three principles underlie the basics of tablesetting techniques. Of prime importance is cleanliness: table utensils must be kept clean and polished. Second is appropriateness. However much one may wish to combine elements of different traditions, it won't do to encourage major violations of accepted styles, like eating *sashimi* with a fork. For maximum ease in eating, Chinese food should be eaten Chinese style, and Japanese food Japanese style. By the same token, when serving other regional dishes, one should be willing to follow custom, including eating with the hands, when appropriate. Third involves aesthetic considerations. It is important to take pains to satisfy all five senses.

Keeping the above guidelines in mind, let us consider some specific points to establish clearly when planning tablesettings. First, *time*. In what season and time period will the occasion take place? Is the meal to be served in the morning, at noon, or at night? Second, *place* and *setting*. What country or region will serve as the theme setting? Will it be in a room, outdoors, or in a corner of a restaurant? Third is *purpose*. Why are people being brought together to share a meal? Is it a personal celebration of some kind, or a seasonal custom? Next comes the *menu* and *tableware*. The menu should be determined by time, place, and occasion, and the table utensils should take into account all elements contributing to the total effect, including flowers and lighting.

Another important point to remember is that the setting should be planned with the people in mind, for they play the central role. People should feel comfortable and be able to appreciate the total dining experience. A tablesetting is truly finished only when food and people are present. Some settings seem to lose their point when people sit down to eat, which is a pity. Also, one must consider the relation of the table to its surrounding space, and its balance with the decor. Finally, the tableware must be arranged properly. It is not

Costly wares enrich a tablesetting

A setting suited to the time, place, and occasion

A flower arrangement lends impact to the dining space

appropriate to seek special effects by arranging the dishes in random order, or facing backwards, for example. Japanese dishes, and any others with a definite front and back, must be lined up properly.

These are basic tablesetting techniques. When arranging a crossover setting, certain other points must be kept in mind. A crossover setting should be dramatic. It should have maximum impact, and it should tell a story or inspire a dream. At the same time, overdoing the effort can make the tablesetting seem forced. One must know how far to go.

Specifically, two basic techniques are often involved. One, which works best with casual and ethnic styles, is to base the presentation on *repetition*. Use the same items, colors, or textures over and over, to achieve a direct impact.

Table utensils arranged in a distinctive repeating pattern

The other technique, which works well in conjunction with Western *classic* and *elegant* styles, is to base the arrangement on *distinctiveness*. Dramatic effects can be obtained by using costly wares, valuable wares, or wares of the sort that illuminate the table by their very presence. The history of a utensil, or a story associated with its maker, can provide the background for pleasant mealtime conversation.

A Japanese space employing straight-lined components

SPACE AND TABLETOPS

Leading the eyes upward in an European setting

There is a close connection between a tablesetting and its surrounding space. Suppose you were designing a tablesetting combining elements of Japanese, European, and Chinese styles. For a Japanese setting with a European influence, a relatively narrow space is desirable. In all other combinations, a wider space is necessary.

A purely European setting requires a high ceiling, leading the eye up and up. The space above and around the table should be as wide as possible. Western table utensils are designed to fit into such wide spaces.

The implements used in formal Chinese settings are almost all created from the imperial tradition, so most are extravagant. Utensils decorated with vivid colors and complicated designs are well suited to the vast spaces of an imperial palace. Lavish rooms decorated in sumptuous style, with lots of vermilion, gold, and green, are ideal.

Pure Japanese style, by contrast, suggests the narrow world of the tea ceremony room. The dishes used for formal tea ceremony dining are the height of good taste, designed with great attention to detail. *Kageurushi* or "shadow lacquer," in which the design beneath the lacquer appears only in certain lighting, is a style of utensil that goes well with the small space of a tea room. Many Japanese utensils have a delicate grace and beauty which is well set off in a traditional Japanese room among the straight-lined components of *tatami*, *shoji*, square pillars, and the like. Conversely, within the highly decorated interior of a rococo European room, for example, such utensils would be overwhelmed and completely out of place. The bright, ornamental utensils which originated in the merchant culture of the Edo period (1600–1868), however, are more at home out of doors, or in some other spacious setting, than in a restricted environment like that of a tea room.

The peculiar balance between a table and its surrounding space thus relies on historical circumstances as well as on individual tastes of beauty. In fact, the table designs of a given era can easily be imagined by examining the architecture and interior decoration of the room (or outdoor space, as the case may be) in which dining took place.

For formal Chinese settings: a spacious room

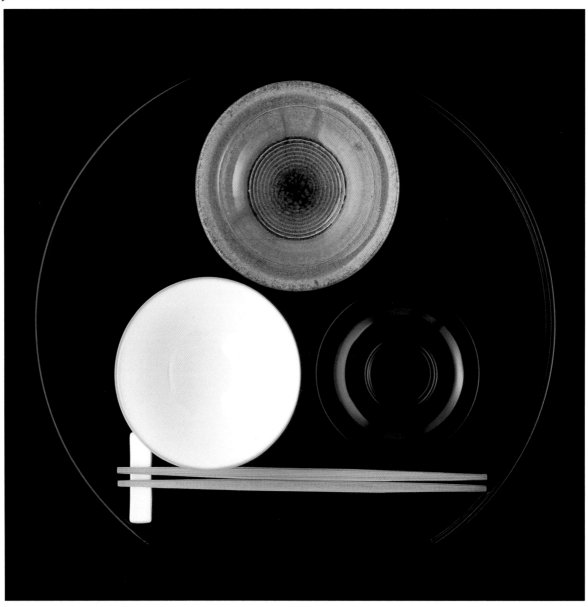

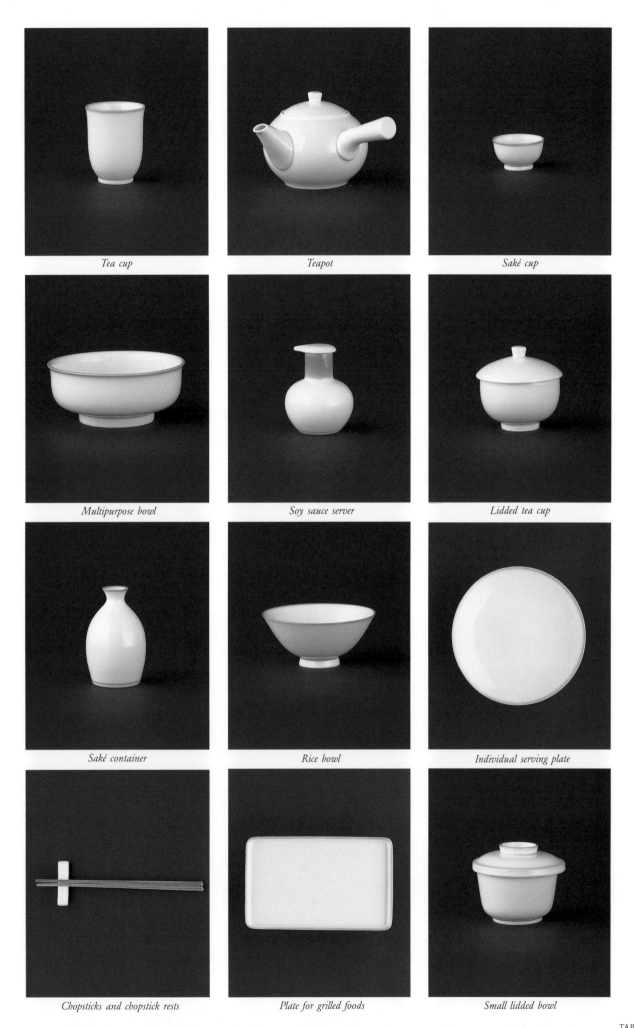

Tea cup

Teapot

Saké cup

Multipurpose bowl

Soy sauce server

Lidded tea cup

Saké container

Rice bowl

Individual serving plate

Chopsticks and chopstick rests

Plate for grilled foods

Small lidded bowl

JAPANESE TABLEWARE

Japanese-style tableware can be broadly divided into two types: *haré* and *ke*. The first is appropriate for any auspicious, gala occasion, the second for any ordinary, everyday occasion.

Haré utensils, or formal ware, are vessels designed to hold specific types of food on special occasions, as epitomized in the philosophy and works of Rosanjin. *Ke* utensils, or informal ware, on the other hand, are characterized best by the folkcraft philosophy of Yanagi, which emphasizes utility and function, and can be used to serve a variety of foods.

Standards for selecting the two types of tableware also differ. *Haré* dishes, including formal, high-quality lacquerware, dishes of conventional shape, Kyoto ware porcelain, and the like, are chosen according to strict standards. *Ke* utensils, however, need only be sturdy; they may be of any shape, however playful, and may draw on a wide variety of types including stoneware and earthenware.

To appreciate the esthetics of Japanese dinnerware, it is best to understand the standards used for measuring the size of dishes. Basically, the human body provides the scale against which the size of Japanese utensils is measured. *Zokujinki* are vessels whose length is one-tenth the stature of a full-grown adult; *mihabamono* are trays approximately the width of a pair of human shoulders. Bowls are made to fit the size of a circle described by placing the middle fingers and thumbs of each hand together. This standard produces bowls of two sizes, 8 and 15 centimeters in diameter, as well as dishes 30 or 40 centimeters across.

The following are the most useful dishes to acquire for home use: for formal *haré* utensils, lacquerware, Kyoto ware porcelain dishes for sashimi, lidded Kyoto ware bowls, and plates for appetizers; for *ke* utensils, large platters, rice bowls, teacups, small bowls, and individual small plates (15 centimeters in diameter).

In collecting signed pieces, or works from various kilns, it is important to match them according to size. Even if the materials and designs of the dishes are all different, as long as they match in size, there is no disharmony in using them together. Other important points to keep in mind are how well the dishes stack together, how easy they are to carry, and whether they are the right size to hold in comfort. Unlike Western dishes, Japanese dishes are often held in the hand while eating, so such considerations are important.

Decorative ware for use on special occasions

For informal, everyday use: casual *tableware*

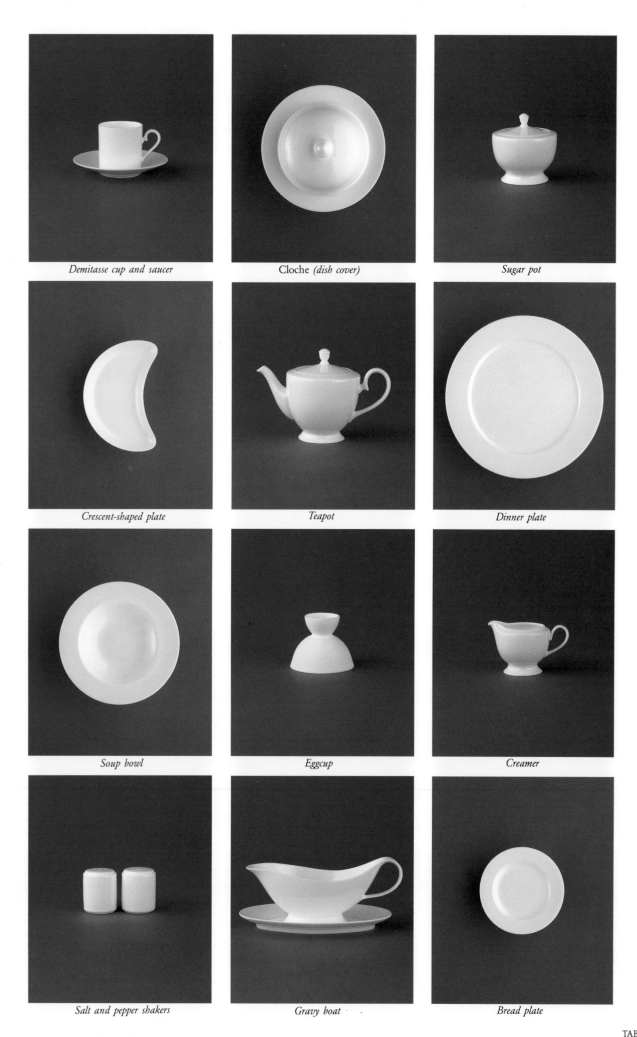

Demitasse cup and saucer

Cloche *(dish cover)*

Sugar pot

Crescent-shaped plate

Teapot

Dinner plate

Soup bowl

Eggcup

Creamer

Salt and pepper shakers

Gravy boat

Bread plate

WESTERN TABLEWARE

Tableware used on special occasions in the West falls into four general categories. First are what may be called *classic* dishware, including English porcelain and bone china, gold-dusted dishes evoking the Victorian era, heavily decorated, almost rococo dishes, stressing ornamentation and sumptuousness. Naturally these are most often used at formal dinners and similar events. Next is what may be called *elegant* plates, showing the influence of French Limoges porcelain in their characteristic designs of handpainted leaves and flowers or Egyptian motifs popular in the Napoleonic era. Again, these are primarily for formal occasions. Dishware that may be termed *casual* is primarily made up of American and country-style stoneware and porcelain, often with playful designs featuring basket-weave patterns or wildflowers. These are ideal for informal daytime events. *Modern*, or contemporary-design, dishware, often from Italy, Scandinavia, or Germany, is noted for clean lines and minimal ornamentation, and is made of a variety of materials, including porcelain, pottery and even metal. Many signed pieces by current designers can be found in this category.

To collect *classic* and *elegant* Western dishes for the home, one begins with a dinner set: dinner plates, 25 to 27 centimeters in diameter; fish (or salad) plates 21 to 25 centimeters in diameter; cake (or salad) plates 17 to 19 centimeters in diameter; bread-and-butter plates approximately 16 centimeters in diameter; rimmed soup bowls; bouillon cups and saucers; and coffee cups and saucers. It might be wise to start with dinner plates and salad plates, and gradually add on other dishes in the same pattern.

Collecting and mixing dishes of different patterns can also be fun, but in this case it is important to match the tone of white used, since dishes with different tones of white generally clash. Large dinner plates (25–27 centimeters in diameter) with a bold pattern can be combined with other dishes as service plates. The smaller dish set on top should be as simple as possible, so that a variety of foods can be served. Coffee cups and saucers should be as gay and showy as possible, since they represent the finale of the meal.

For *casual* utensils, one should collect large plates, bowls, and rimmed soup bowls. These can be handy for serving pasta and salad; matched with large cups and saucers, they can be used easily for breakfast as well. Large plates mix well with Japanese ceramics and Oriental metal utensils.

Among *modern* dishes, the basic requirements are large plates 25 to 27 centimeters in diameter; medium-sized plates 17 to 21 centimeters in diameter; and cups and saucers. Using unique tableware of modern Italian design as accents during a course can produce interesting effects. It is good to bear in mind that modern wares do not marry well with decorative wares of the European *classic* or *elegant* tradition. They actually blend more congenially with Japanese wares. Japanese cuisine also goes surprisingly well with modern wares; sushi, for example, is nicely complemented by Italian contemporary style.

Modern *tableware with a contemporary design from Scandinavia*

Classic *tableware: English porcelain*

Casual *tableware with playful designs*

Elegant *tableware with a delicate, soft image*

CHINESE TABLEWARE

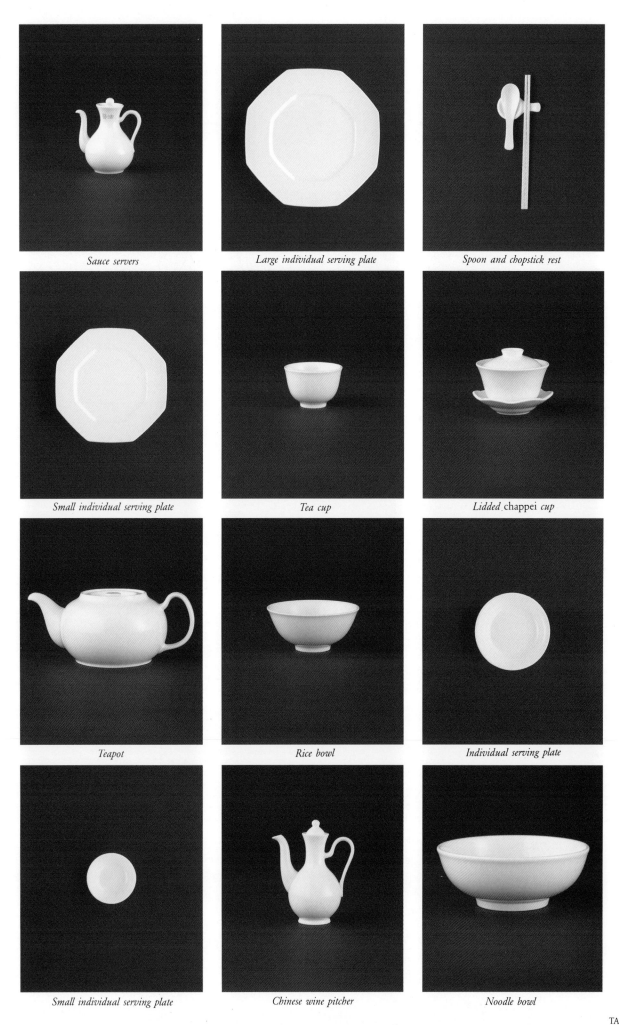

Sauce servers

Large individual serving plate

Spoon and chopstick rest

Small individual serving plate

Tea cup

Lidded chappei cup

Teapot

Rice bowl

Individual serving plate

Small individual serving plate

Chinese wine pitcher

Noodle bowl

CHINESE TABLEWARE

Chinese tableware can be divided broadly into new and old. The latter includes traditional utensils used to serve Chinese imperial cuisine; they are highly decorative and colorful, with overall designs of red, green, yellow, black, and other vivid colors. Metal utensils are usually gold plated. Such utensils of a bygone era are most attractive when used and enjoyed at formal Chinese occasions.

The last few years have seen new trends in Chinese tableware. *Hsin-p'ai ao-ts'ai*, or Cantonese nouvelle cuisine, has inspired the use of a new style of dishes. The dishes are simple in both color and design, with modern patterns using straight lines or single motifs. These dishes can be used like Western tableware.

The first dishes to look for when starting a collection of Chinese tableware are slightly deep dishes 12–15 centimeters in diameter; soup plates (for rice or soup) approximately 8 centimeters in diameter; teacups for Chinese tea; and chopstick and spoon rests. These four elements are the most basic, although large platters, serving plates, and large bowls are also useful. Until now Chinese tableware has always been represented by deep-dish plates and bowls, but lately shallower, Western-style dishes are also becoming popular. In place of deep Chinese-style bowls, a crossover mood can be struck with Western soup tureens, or Thai lidded bowls. It is also enjoyable to mix old-style Chinese tableware with decorative wares in the Western *classical* and *elegant* traditions.

A soup tureen in the Hsin-p'ai ao-ts'ai-*inspired style*

A new image: Western tableware with Oriental designs

Teacups inspired by traditional Chinese cuisine

Spring

Summer

Autumn

Winter

COLOR SCHEMES

A crossover mood can be subtly evoked through the use of color. Following are some examples showing how careful selection and combination of colors can produce dramatic effects on the table. At the same time, techniques for emphasizing the season can serve as the basis for experimenting with various color schemes.

In playing on spring, *peony* (deep pink) and *purple* provide an appropriately springlike combination of deep colors. This traditional color combination (going all the way back to the Japanese twelve-layered ceremonial kimonos [*juni-hitoe*]) conveys an opulence suggestive of the wealthy merchant princes of the Edo period (1600–1868) in Japan. The table arrangement should be decorative; an evening setting, with dim lighting, is especially effective. It is important not to overdo the use of purple; the ratio of peony to purple should be 8:2. Pale yellowish-green makes a good accent color.

For lighter spring hues, try *pale pink, grass green,* and *pale purple*. This is the classically refined image of spring dating from the Japanese Heian period (794–1185). Because these elegant colors are well set off by natural lighting, they are recommended for a spring breakfast or luncheon. They are beautiful when used in equal proportions; accent colors can be added by using deeper shades of these same colors in smaller proportions (10–20 percent). Furthermore, the proportions can be altered to vary the sense of season: more grass green in early spring, more pale purple in May, and so on.

To emphasize summer, a color scheme based on deep colors of *orange, green,* and *yellow* works well in summertime. These colors are especially appropriate for an Oriental-style table, and used with brightly-colored tableware, such as traditional Chinese dishes in primary hues, they produce a pleasingly quiet harmony. They also go well with decorative Western tableware of the *classic* tradition. The main point to

remember is to use green and yellow liberally, and orange sparingly, as an accent. For a particularly strong presentation of summer, red may be used in place of orange, but it should be held to a ratio of 1:10.

To express summer through lighter colors, try *blue* and *white*, a refreshing color combination suggestive of the sea in summer. Combining white with different gradations of blue evokes a number of interesting effects. Blue and white go well with Japanese utensils such as Imari underglaze blue, and with contemporary-style German or Scandinavian utensils as well. These colors are easy to use but can become monotonous; to add variety, provide a bit of contrast with yellow or red (in a ratio of 1:10 or less), or a deeper blue (at least four shades darker than the main color).

Dark brown and *red* are deep colors suggesting autumn. The key to using them successfully lies in the careful selection and use of the red, a color that includes a wide spectrum of shades from wine red to vermilion; it is worth taking pains to find just the right one. This color scheme goes well with *classic* Western dinnerware and Japanese ceramics, and is highly suitable for evening. At a dinner with subdued lighting, these colors create a sophisticated mood. Due care must be given to the balance of the colors. Olive green works well as an accent.

For light autumn colors, use *beige* and *salmon pink*. The French language contains many words signifying various shades of beige, from the dappled spots

Peony, purple, and black combine to portray a stylish harmony

Right: Cherry blossom pink and pale flower designs produce a refined image

of a fawn to melted milk chocolate, and indeed a color scheme based on beige has an aura of Parisian elegance. Western dinnerware of the *elegant* tradition and Japanese Kyoto ware porcelain, accordingly, go well with such a table-setting. These colors, also used in traditional Kyoto confections, are considered extremely sophisticated. To prevent them from blurring, accent the setting with dark brown, olive green, or tea green.

For winter, *deep tones of gold, red*, and *green* work well. These are the traditional colors of Christmas, and they also correspond to the colors of over-glaze enamel wares and gold-painted porcelain in Japan; such a color scheme thus creates an atmosphere of luxury and splendor. The beauty of the colors blends well with black lacquerware and formal Western dinnerware. The colors are set off to advantage by indoor fluorescent lighting, and candlelight plays up the gold. To avoid gaudiness, use of gold should be understated. The color comes in all shades from the most subdued to a bright reddish-gold; care must be exercised in choosing the appropriate shade and using it judiciously. For an accent color, black or navy is best.

Light gray, wisteria (lavender), and *cinnabar red* are light tones that evoke winter. These colors, taken from the traditional "48 browns and 100 grays" sequence of muted colors, have a subtle beauty that is smart and sophisticated. They go well with Japanese tableware, of course, with Western *elegant* dishes, and with *modern* Italian wares as well. The shade of gray must be selected with particular care. A muddy gray will spoil the overall effect, so a sober, translucent shade should be sought. For an accent color, use a tiny bit of black or dark brown, no more than one or two percent of the whole. For example, small plates of cinnabar red could be set on larger gray service plates, on a wisteria-hued tablecloth; in this case, the napkins might be tied with dark brown ribbons.

Brown, black, and gold combine for a decorative display

A refreshing combination: white and gradations of blue

Combining brown, black, lavender, and gray

Lacquer and Silver

Handcrafted Paper and Lacquer

Lacquer and Brass

Silver and Lacquer

Lacquer and Glass

Silk Crepe and Lacquer

COMBINATIONS OF MATERIALS

Effective combinations of unusual materials can create a brand-new ambience on the table. Consider the following examples.

Bamboo and Acrylic

When using bamboo, the goal is to bring out the three-dimensional quality of the joints, and the brightness of the natural green color. For acrylic, emphasis should be on the material's transparency. Keeping these points in mind, bamboo and acrylic can be combined in many pleasing ways. These two materials, one natural and the other man-made, have an unexpected affinity for each other.

Segments of bamboo split lengthwise can be lined up, with acrylic slabs on top. Acrylic boxes can be filled with water to float or stand green bamboo. Any combination of these two should bring out the linear beauty of the materials as well as the transparency of acrylic, and would go well with a modern theme.

Stainless Steel and Lacquer

Stainless steel, with its air of modernity and coldness, and lacquerware, with its air of tradition and warmth, would seem to be two materials with nothing in common, but they share two surprising qualities: luster and reflection. Despite obvious differences in the way they shine and reflect light, both materials bring out the beauty of the play of light on surfaces.

Set a lacquered bowl on a stainless steel tray to appreciate the reflection of the bowl's design, or an Old Imari antique on a stainless steel tray to enjoy the contrast of old and new.

Silk Crepe and Ceramics

Silk crepe (*chirimen*), a refined, traditional Japanese material, has a unique texture and feel. Earthenware utensils, in contrast, have a dynamic, casual image, and a characteristically rough texture. The interesting tactile variations of these two materials forms the point of contact between them, and the basis for using them together.

Suppose the setting for a meal includes a Scandinavian wooden tray with earthenware dishes. Alone, these convey a rough, wild impression. Silk crepe napkins complement the roughness of the dishes while adding a touch of elegance, for an entirely different effect. Silk crepe can also be used as a cushion between earthenware and another type of material, such as stainless steel.

Lacquer and silver combined as tableware

Linen and ceramic

Paper and Stone

Both paper and stone are apparently simple, even primitive materials, but in combination they can produce quite modern and elegant results.

The characteristics of paper are translucence and foldability. Stone, while limited by size and shape, offers appealing texture. Simply designed, contemporary tablewares are apt to be beautiful but cold; the addition of paper adds a suggestion of warmth and softness. For Oriental or ethnic table arrangements, the addition of stone deepens the sense of nature or primitiveness.

Paper and stone can also be used with great effectiveness in Japanese-style arrangements, as by setting stones on folded sheets of handcrafted paper (*washi*) for chopstick rests, or piling small stones on handcrafted paper to hold flowers.

Porcelain ceramic wares on handcrafted paper

Acrylic and cut glass

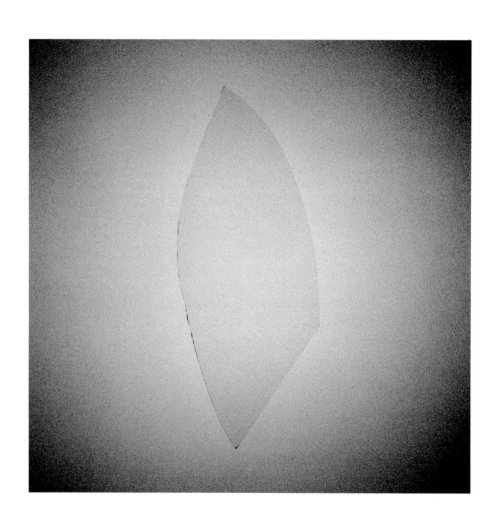

CHAPTER 4
TABLESETTING ELEMENTS

Bamboo and pottery

THE SIGNIFICANCE AND ROLE OF MATERIALS

A firm grasp of the various characteristics of different materials allows one to enjoy the mental stimulation of a tablesetting that appeals to all five senses.

For example, the tableware should be chosen for its suitability in presenting the food. The visual impact of the utensils used will cause subtle differences in flavor.

The visual appeal of a tablesetting is naturally affected by the materials used. A utensil set on a tray of stainless steel, for example, casts a reflection on the tray. Light flickers on the surface of lacquer bowls. Transparent acrylic trays set on cloth placemats let the beauty of the cloth show through. Taking advantage of such interplay between materials can create a sense of anticipation.

The main elements that stir the sense of smell are flowers and the aroma of the food itself. Certain table utensils can provide a pleasant fragrance without affecting the taste of the meal, such as cedar trays and chopsticks, leaves used as plates, or twigs as chopstick rests.

A tablesetting can stimulate the sense of touch by including articles of rough texture, such as earthenware, cloth, and paper; cold, smooth utensils of glass or stainless steel; the soft warmth of wood and lacquerware. This effect can be gained not only from direct physical contact, but from looking at them and imagining how they feel.

To stimulate the sense of hearing one need not always come up with actual sounds; it is important rather to construct a setting that can suggest such sounds as the rustle of paper, the swish of silk, or the silent, wordless play of dish against dish.

An understanding of the meaning and role played by different materials makes it possible to combine them so as to appeal to the senses in various ways. The possibilities for contrast are endless: bright and subdued, strong and mild, festive and quiet, hard and soft, cold and warm. Set your imagination free!

Following are descriptions of traditional Japanese crafted materials: lacquerware, bamboo and wood, handcrafted paper, cloth, glassware, metal, pottery, and porcelain.

Making a pure, clean statement with bamboo, crystal, and linen

LACQUERWARE

Lacquer is quintessentially Japanese to the extent that it has even become known in English as "japanware." Yet lacquer is by no means unique to Japan; it also has a long history in China, Thailand, Vietnam, and many other Asian countries.

The use of lacquerware grew out of a desire to enhance the durability and beauty of wooden utensils. Gradually the method of applying the sap of the lacquer tree was utilized for decorative purposes, and large numbers of lacquered articles began to be made, many for use in religious rites.

The two main colors characteristic of Japanese lacquerware are vermilion and black. These are traditional colors, but they remain fresh and eye-catchingly modern even today. Moreover, finely decorated lacquerware enhances the most gorgeous setting.

There are a number of traditional methods of decorating lacquer, notably *maki-e* (literally "sprinkled-picture"), which involves sprinkling gold or silver dust on liquid lacquer, and mother-of-pearl inlay.

Japanese utensils are often classified according to the traditional system of *shin* (true form), *gyo* (running form), and *so* (grass form). Lacquerware too can be divided this way, with round, vermilion lacquerware corresponding to the very formal *shin* category; and black, slightly irregular lacquerware to the second, less formal, category; and highly decorated wares (using *maki-e* and mother-of-pearl inlay) of irregular shapes (tree leaves, flowers, gold coins, etc) to the third, least formal, category.

Lacquerware has many distinctive characteristics. It is functionally superior because it breathes, and can be used to hold cooked foods without loss of moisture or heat; soups and stews stay piping hot in lacquer bowls, and sandwiches in lacquer boxes remain at the proper temperature without drying out. These qualities should be put to good use.

Of the wide variety of lacquerware shapes, I recommend two in particular: lacquered lunch-boxes, and nested boxes (*ireko*), which can be used in many ways at picnics and parties.

An arrangement of lacquer bowls; the two at top right display excellent examples of maki-e.

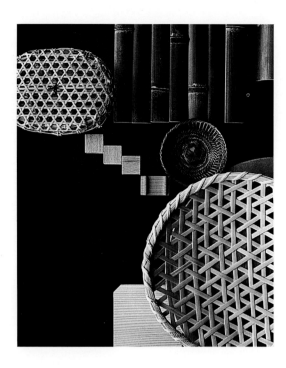

BAMBOO AND WOOD

Among all tableware materials, bamboo and wood are the most versatile, both wild enough to capture the scent of the outdoors with their primal fragrance, yet sophisticated enough to adorn the finest table.

Bamboo is used widely throughout Asia, in Thailand, the Philippines, and China as well as in Japan. In Japan it has been in daily use as tableware for many centuries. There are all kinds of bamboo table utensils, including large, open baskets, close-woven ones with fitted lids, trays, and so on. Bamboo baskets vary greatly in weave, color, and design—types of weave range from rough openwork to fine wickerwork, while colors range from bright green to brown. Novel effects can be achieved by lining woven bamboo utensils with handcrafted paper (*washi*), or coating them with lacquer.

Traditional kinds of wood used for table utensils in Japan include cedar, cypress, cherry, and beech, as well as teak and sandalwood. These different types of wood are prized for their distinctive grain, color, and fragrance. It's worth noting that cypress also helps keep food from spoiling.

Bamboo and wood utensils are used most effectively not as the main elements of a tablesetting, but as accessories. For example, dishes for one course of a meal might be served on cedar boards, or large bamboo baskets might be used in place of trays at a buffet. Used as an accent in this way, wood and bamboo work well to make a crossover tablesetting.

Materials should be chosen with an eye to the season, as well; in spring, for example, green bamboo is best, and in fall, cedar or sooted bamboo. Mixing in Thai or Vietnamese basketry can lend food an especially exotic air.

Clockwise from center: cedar napkin rings, mutsume *woven bamboo basket, green bamboo tray, bamboo tea saucer, pine tray, large* mutsume *woven basket, cedar board.*

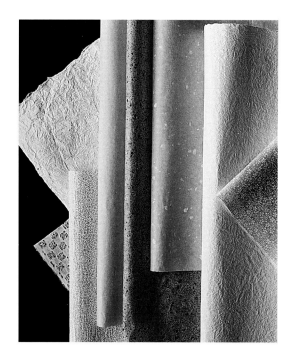

HANDCRAFTED PAPER (*WASHI*)

In many countries paper is considered an informal material, but in Japan handcrafted paper often conveys an impression of the highest luxury.

There are all sorts of *washi*, including super-thin sheets, sheets containing gold powder, figured sheets, translucent sheets, crepe paper, and more. In design *washi* may be fine-patterned, striped, interwoven with gold or silver thread, imprinted with cherry blossoms or with fall leaves. Some types are delicate and fancy, others earthy and rough to the touch. There is in fact an unimaginable variety of *washi*.

Depending on the way it is crafted, *washi* may be suited to an auspicious occasion, such as a wedding, or it may express condolence. Current uses in Japan have evolved from bygone days, when particular *washi* patterns were a clue to the user's social status. Traditional styles existed for everyone from country samurai to young ladies of the town.

In tablesettings, handcrafted paper may be used in a variety of roles: *Washi* may serve as a divider between two utensils, or it may line a plate in place of lace-paper. It may be used to wrap food, or serve as placemat, menu, or namecard. *Washi* may even function as a fork or knife rest, or chopstick rest. Its uses are limited only by one's imagination.

Combining handcrafted paper from various other countries is another way to increase the enjoyment of a crossover tablesetting. Besides *washi* in the same tablesetting, using heavy Indian or Thai paper as doilies, or using inscribed Korean paper to serve cookies, can produce a striking effect.

When selecting *washi*, it is important to choose a color that blends well with those of the utensils and other elements of the setting. Insist on the finest quality *washi* available. Show off *washi*'s unique translucent beauty by wrapping it around candles like a lantern, or folding sheets of *washi* over autumn leaves so that the colors of the leaves show through.

Be careful, though, not to go overboard. The natural beauty of Japanese handcrafted paper is best brought out by its use as an accent rather than in large amounts.

Assorted varieties of washi, *showing a diversity of colors and textures.*

CLOTH

Fabrics are an important medium for lending variety to tablesettings. Simply changing a white tablecloth to a red one, for example, completely transforms the atmosphere. Textiles have the power to stir drama and interest, by contrasting with or complementing plate colors, or by mixing colors and patterns.

In the West, tablecloths have traditionally been made of such materials as linen, damask, cotton, or synthetics. If we stretch our imagination, however, other possibilities present themselves. Thai silk, pongee, or crepe; fine hempen cloth (*jofu*); Indian chintz or satin damask: these and other fine textiles from throughout the world can be used to express the crossover spirit. Indian chintz may be made of either hemp or cotton, and Thai silk can be plain, patterned, or gold-embroidered, lined with gauze or unlined, damask, or any of a variety of types. In addition to color and pattern variations, they can provide a variety of tactile sensations, a heightened sense of season, or a touch of elegance.

In choosing a material, proper attention should first be given to texture. Cloths with a rough, nubbly, or other interesting surface can provide a pleasantly stimulat-ing effect. Pay attention, too, to the cloth's seasonal emphasis. Just as light material is used for midsummer clothing, so tablecloths should be selected according to thickness, patterns, and material to create a heightened sense of the season.

Third, it is useful to remember that textiles and patterns help create specific moods, from the most informal to highly aristocratic. For example, try combining crepe and damask for a formal atmosphere, pongee and itak (*kasuri*) for a more casual touch, wave-pattern cloth and lined silk for a traditional, yet stylish look.

Cloth can be used as tablecloth or placemat as well as wrapping. Lacquer boxes wrapped in colorful cloths are the equivalent of European-style glass *cloches* in Japanese terms. (The pleasure of unwrapping and opening the box enhances the enjoyment of eating.) In addition, decorative effects can be achieved by twisting cloths into interesting shapes, or piling them up to support a soup tureen or other utensil.

Clockwise from left: hand towel, hemp printed in a lattice design, pongee, silk crepe with cherry blossom design, silk crepe, silk pongee, yorokedan-patterned silk crepe. Center: kimono silk cloths.

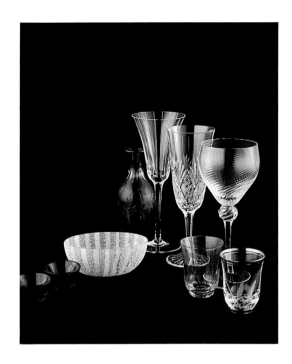

GLASSWARE

In Western tablesettings, glassware adds light and dimension to the table. A flat tablesetting of Western utensils is brightened immediately by depth and sparkle.

In Japan, glassware traditionally has had other important functions. One is creating a sense of the season. Along with water and ice, glass dishes and bowls are an excellent prop for a summer presentation. Conversely, they are never used in winter.

Glassware also conveys a sense of luxury. All varieties of Japanese glass were originally imported, from early Dutch *diamant* and Portuguese *vidro* to cut glass and Tyrolean. Back in the Edo period (1600–1868), for example, glass products were rare and precious. To this day glass containers for Japanese food can convey an extremely luxurious impression; many are made with gold dust or elaborate faceting.

Another distinctive feature of Japanese glassware is the large variety of unusual shapes. In Japan there are many items of striking shape or design, including small glasses for chilled wine, saké cups, bowls, large plates. Furthermore, Japanese utensils are commonly adorned with sumptuous decoration of a sort used chiefly on vases and the like in the West, including gravure, cut glass, stained glass, and designs of gold and other colors. Thus, Japanese glassware tends to be used in ones or twos, more as a lavish accent rather than as part of multiple placesettings.

In Japan it is important to choose one distinctive type of glass piece for a tablesetting. Glass is also used for chilled bowls, plates of *sashimi*, chopstick rests, and lidded table utensils. A glass utensil filled with water makes a pleasant, summery decoration, or designed with gold dust and set atop a black lacquer tray it makes an elegant statement.

Left to right: saké cups, venetian-inspired bowl, kiriko *cut glass saké container, wine glass, cut glass, venetian wine glass, saké cups with gold design.*

METAL

In the West, the highest quality metal tableware is sterling silver. European silver utensils are equivalent to Japanese lacquerware: Silver is a material with the weight of tradition, to be passed along from generation to generation as a family heirloom. A treasured silver candelabrum occupies the same position in a European family as a treasured set of tiered lacquer boxes in a Japanese family.

In planning crossover settings, metalwares generally come much less into play than they do on purely Western tables. Lately, however, a new eclecticism has appeared, making effective use of metal. It is a good idea to find ways to combine metal utensils with other materials in a tablesetting—not to evoke tradition but simply to have fun.

The main metals used in Japanese tablesetting are gold and silver, including gold-and-silver-plated metals. Also popular are copper, brass, tin, iron, stainless steel, and platinum. Gold, silver, and platinum are formal and elegant, copper casual, brass and tin Oriental in tone.

The metals may be processed in any of a number of ways, for a matte finish, a mirrorlike finish, or a hairline finish with many narrow lines. The technique used to finish the material determines the mood it expresses.

On the table, metal utensils must always be treated as accents for the setting. On a Western table, silver vessels are meant to blend in easily with others, but for a crossover mood, metal utensils should serve only as added interest. For example, brass and tin can be used for an Oriental touch. A silver bowl can hold nuts or fried foods set on a sheet of handcrafted paper, and a lidded silver dish can contain some unexpectedly exotic food.

Clockwise from center: silver condiment container, silver-plated plate, silver-plated cups, sterling silver plate, pewter plate, brass tray, pewter plate, brass bowl.

POTTERY AND PORCELAIN

At first glance, pottery and porcelain may seem alike but there are great differences between them. The most significant difference is in the temperature of the final firing. A low final temperature produces an opaque ware of relatively rough, porous quality, which gives out a low, dull sound when struck; this is known as pottery. Porcelain is made with a high final firing temperature, so that the surface is smooth and non-porous. Porcelain wares are translucent and produce a clear, ringing sound when struck.

Japanese pottery and porcelain wares vary considerably from region to region. Here we will consider a few of the most representative types.

First, Arita ware. This is a type of porcelain made in northern Kyushu; exported to Europe in the 17th century from the port of Imari, it became known to the world as Imari ware. Some of the representative types are blue and white *sometsuke* wares, red and gold painted porcelain (*kinrande*), and wares decorated with scenes of plants and gardens, known as *kakiemon*. Arita ware goes well with most Western utensils, especially English bone china.

Kiyomizu ware, a thin porcelain made in Kyoto, was originally used by aristocrats at the tea ceremony, and even today it is often used at formal *kaiseki* meals. It is advisable to match it with delicate Limoges or fine Meissen ware.

Kutani ware, a porcelain made in Ishikawa Prefecture, is noted for its colorful, intricate style. Kutani ware makes a dramatic statement on the table; like Bernard Palissy's rustic creations in the West, it should be given center stage.

Bizen ware is a type of unglazed pottery made in Okayama Prefecture. The designs produced by flames wrapping themselves around the wares are particularly admired. Bizen ware goes well with modern Italian, German, or Scandinavian tableware.

Oribe ware was developed by the celebrated tea master Hotta Oribe (1544–1615); it is characterized by paintings of autumn grasses and other plants on a green glaze. Much Oribe ware is the work of renowned potters, and Oribe ware is often used as tea utensils. Its striking individuality makes it valuable as an accent in tablesetting.

Mashiko ware is an informal type of pottery produced in Tochigi Prefecture. Strongly associated with folkcrafts and

decorative art, it is characterized by powerful, simple large bowls and teapots. This ware was introduced to the West by potters Bernard Leach (1887–1979) and Hamada Shoji (1894–1978). In combination with brass, Scandinavian woodcraft, and Southern French ceramics, it produces a tablesetting full of warmth.

Many Asian countries, beginning with China and Korea, produce pottery and porcelain of the highest quality. Chinese blue and white porcelain and Korean celadon are preeminent examples of the finest tradition in Asian ceramics, and have had a correspondingly large influence. As crossroads of East and West, moreover, such countries as Vietnam, Thailand, India, and Burma exhibit intriguing combinations of ceramic styles. A Persian-style shape paired with a Chinese-style pattern, for example, gives a direct sense of eclecticism at work in the history of tableware culture.

Unlike the West, in the East there is enormous variation in the shapes of tableware. Generally, dishes are not created for specific uses, such as a bread-and-butter plate or service platter, but are of great diversity. Tablesettings should take advantage of this variety and bring out the appeal of individual shapes. Japanese tableware should be used to convey a sense of the season through appropriate designs or materials, as by using glassware in the summer and heavy earthenware bowls in the winter.

Opposite: Clockwise from bottom left—Arita ware, Arita ware, Oribe bowl, ceramic tea cup, blue and white lidded container, Bizen ware, Kiseto ware, white celadon bowl, sometsuke *ware. Center:: sometsuke ware.*
Above: Small blue and white porcelain plates
Below: Kutani ceramic ware

CHAPTER 5

PRACTICAL INFORMATION

Old Seto ware paired with green bamboo and flowers as a champagne cooler for a special occasion

PREPARATIONS

Certain techniques are required for a tablesetting to move from image to reality. In this section I will give a detailed account of some indispensable tablesetting techniques, but first, let us consider the steps involved in staging a party.

The first thing to do when inviting guests over is to decide on a theme, and then plan a guest list accordingly. Apart from basic themes related to the season, other possibilities include travel memories, anniversaries, homage to an artist or writer, or special effects with music or light—themes which impart a story to the table. Once the theme is chosen, you should draw up a list of appropriate guests.

Next is the sending out of invitations. For a formal occasion, they should go out a month to three weeks ahead of time; otherwise, from two weeks to ten days is about right. The cards should be made in the spirit of the chosen theme, so in a sense the tablesetting actually begins here. If cherry blossoms are the theme of the occasion, for example, prepare cards of pale pink *washi*. This allows the guests to plan what clothes to wear and what gifts to bring, in accordance with that spirit.

A week ahead of time, draw up a rough schedule for the party. Begin now to contact the florist, arrange transportation, work out the menu, and select appropriate utensils. Hors d'oeuvres and beverages should be planned so as to provide a variety of selections for guests. Minimize fuss during the party by incorporating cuisine that can be prepared ahead of time, such as baked, roasted, and stewed foods, into the menu.

Six days ahead of time, begin preliminary food preparation. Once the menu is decided on, start with the foods to be pickled or stewed, and work out any necessary arrangements with caterers. Utensils of silver or lacquer should be polished and aired, and the tablecloth washed and ironed.

Five days ahead of time, plan the layout of the room, and do a thorough cleaning. As soon as the arrangement of furniture is decided on, cleaning can begin. Little by little, furniture should be polished, windows washed, and so on, in preparation for the day of the party.

Four days ahead of time, begin planning the details of table-setting and room decoration. Give thought to namecards and menu cards. Change paintings on the wall to complement the party theme. Work out lighting effects and other details of decoration for a balanced spatial presentation.

On the third day before the party, clean out the refrigerator to create enough space for the foods you will need to store. Proceed with shopping for ingredients, selection and coordination of tableware, and order the flowers and plants.

The day before the party, you should begin the preliminary arrangements for cooking, arrange for delivery of the flowers, prepare the entranceway, check candles, do final shopping for ingredients, and lay in a stock of beverages.

On the morning of the party, do a last thorough cleaning, with special attention to the toilet facilities. The arrangement of table and other furniture should also of course be finalized. In the afternoon, begin setting the table and organizing the kitchen. There should be enough room to set out plates to serve food on, and a large garbage container to dispose of waste in the kitchen. Allow plenty of time for beverages to chill. Champagne, for example, should be chilled for two hours before drinking.

Plan the cooking in accordance with the menu. Prepare desserts or other items which need to be chilled early enough.

An hour before the guests are to arrive, carry out a final survey of the tablesetting, flowers, and decoration of the entranceway, and begin dressing for the evening. Thirty to forty minutes beforehand, sprinkle water in the entranceway and light the candles or switch on the lights, and check the hors d'oeuvres and drinks. When all of these steps have been followed, preparations for receiving your guests are complete.

Japanese-style bone china

Western-style Arita ware

FLOWERS

It goes without saying that flowers play an indispensable role in determining the total effect of a tablesetting. Before considering how best to use flowers for a crossover effect, let us first look at the arrangement of flowers in Japanese, Western, Chinese, and other ethnic settings.

In a Japanese setting, flowers play the same role that they do in the tea ceremony, namely, to evoke a sense of the season.

The transparency of crystal illuminates the beauty of white roses and adiantum

Flower and bamboo floating in a water-filled acrylic box

In a Western setting, flowers function in a scheme of total color coordination. The colors of the flowers must harmonize with the tableware and tablecloth, and with each other. The volume and quality of flowers must also be taken into consideration.

In Chinese table arrangements, the symbolic meaning of the flowers comes into play. Flowers are important in the context of a garden or "borrowed scenery," and it is also popular to select flowers for a meal according to Chinese poetry.

For ethnic presentations, the focus might be on beauty of form. Papyrus leaves, reeds and the like can be successfully combined with tropical flowers and wildflowers in exotic, sculptural styles.

The above generalizations can be adapted to arrange flowers in an eclectic, crossover style. For example, flowers traditionally used by the Japanese, such as wisteria, could be presented in a Western context by combining them with a purple tablecloth. Conversely, flowers popularly used in the West, such as spring crocuses and hyacinths, could be used according to a Japanese perspective by arranging them in a lacquer vase. If the basic principles are adhered to, flowers can be arranged freely as the occasion demands, according to the theme of the setting.

The value placed on the flower container varies according to the culture. In the Japanese and Chinese tradition, the container is highly valued, and its historical background, for example, might play an important part in the setting, whereas in the West the flowers are always central. In combining different traditions, however, a more flexible approach to the container is desirable.

One way to give variety to the flower

An arrangement balances a tablesetting

container is to choose something not usually used as a vase. In addition to such Japanese items as lacquer tiered boxes, lacquer bowls, bamboo baskets and the like, why not try a large Egyptian copper platter or a Thai brass bowl? Secondly, natural objects can be used as flower holders; try fashioning containers by splitting bamboo, folding leaves, or piling stones, among other ideas. A novel approach is to experiment with using modern, high-tech items for the purpose: acrylic boxes, stainless steel containers, empty cans, even laboratory decanters or flasks. Sen no Rikyu, the consummate tea master, is said to have amazed his guests on occasion by arranging flowers in a sword scabbard or water bucket; that spirit of playfulness, of seeking the unexpected, is worthy of emulation.

Finally, let us consider the basic points of flower arrangement. Of primary importance is color combination. The value of expensive flowers is diminished if colors are mismatched. Attention must be paid to color coordination of the total surroundings. Balance is also important; the flowers must complement the tableware and surrounding space in both quality and quantity. Always use flowers in season. Local flowers that are just in season will be less expensive, and easily available. Due care must also be given to placement of flowers. The impression they give will vary according to the angle at which they are seen. One way to arrange flowers is to begin at the center and add to the arrangement symmetrically on right and left. When placing an order with a florist, it is wise to have a standing order, to specify a color theme, and to acquaint the florist with your likes and dislikes.

A beautiful flower arrangement frames a soup tureen

Textural emphasis in an exotic symmetrical arrangement

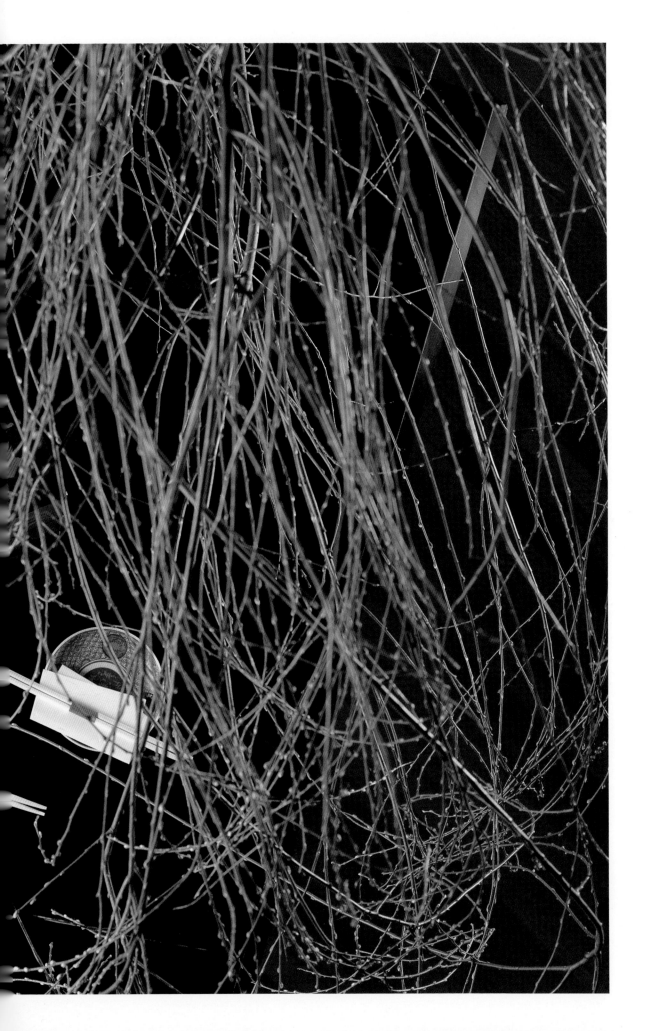

TABLE LINENS

A single tablecloth, along with fresh napkins, placemats, or runner, can completely change the atmosphere of a table. Table linens, as these various cloths are known, play a vital role in tablesettings. Color and texture are the main variables in choosing tablecloths, placemats, and runners, but with napkins, how well they function is also an important consideration. Here let us consider the basic points, and some variations, in the presentation of napkins. Everything that has been said about napkin materials applies to tablecloths as well.

There are five basic materials for napkins. Linen, a material so standard that it has become the generic name for cloths used at table, is the most formal material for napkins. Freshly starched white linen napkins are appropriate for a formal dinner.

Damask napkins, made of fine twill cotton with no colored thread, are second in quality only to linen. The cloth is said to take its name from the ancient Syrian capital of Damascus, where a forebear of modern damask was woven around the 13th century.

Cotton is appropriate for dining at home. Cotton napkins can be either casual, in a variety of colors and patterns, or fancy, with lace or embroidery.

Still more casual are napkins made of synthetic spun fabrics, which can be of any color or pattern, and are easy to launder. They are just right for using anytime at home.

Finally we come to paper napkins, the easiest to use of all. Paper napkins can be enjoyed in all sorts of bold colors, patterns, and shapes. They are recommended as a basic, informal way to become acquainted with the function of a napkin.

Napkin size is another consideration in successful tablesetting. There are presently three main kinds of napkins in use: dinner napkins, 50 (55) centime-ters × 50 (55) centimeters; luncheon or home-use napkins, 40 (45) × 40 (45) centimeters; and teatime napkins, 30 (35) centimeters × 30 (35) centimeters. Cocktail napkins are square (15 centimeters × 15 centimeters) or rectangular (15 centimeters × 18 centimeters).

There are literally hundreds of ways to fold napkins, with colorful names like "bishop's hat," "candle," "fan," and the like. This diversity reflects the history of napkins as they have developed, in the cultural climate of each country.

Let us now examine how napkins and other table linens might be used in a crossover setting.

First, make the most of the sense of touch. Using silk crepe, handcrafted paper, or other material with a distinctive texture adds an Oriental or ethnic touch. Second, experiment freely with unconventional shapes, such as napkins tied in knots or folded and tucked. Experiments with size are another possibility. Small *fukusa*, decorative crepe squares, can be used as cocktail napkins or doilies.

A small fukusa *serves as a doily*

Folding a napkin appropriately for a formal occasion

A tasseled napkin evokes an Oriental image

HOW TO FOLD NAPKINS

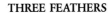

| **SIMPLE SQUARE** | **THREE FEATHERS** | *MUSUBI* |

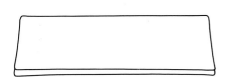

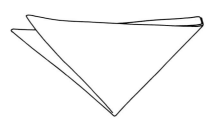

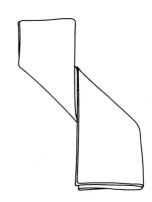

1. Fold lengthwise into thirds to form a long rectangle.

1. Fold diagonally to form a triangle, then fold from one side to the other to form another triangle, slightly off center, with one side overlapping the other, as shown.

1. Fold napkin up lengthwise in quarters. Take lower left corner and fold up along the center line; fold the upper right corner down the same way, as shown.

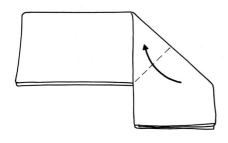

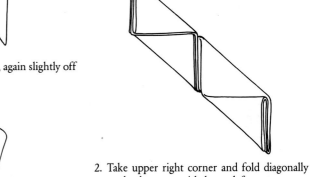

2. Pull upper right corner down to meet the center line.

2. Fold top right corner across, again slightly off center.

2. Take upper right corner and fold diagonally over; do the same with lower left corner.

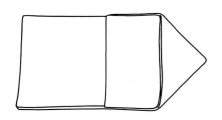

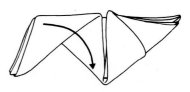

3. Fold lower right edge up to meet the top edge.

3. Take the right edge and fold under, as shown.

3. Take upper point and fold down; take lower point and fold up. Take upper left and lower right points and fold across to meet at the center line.

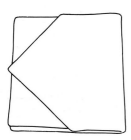

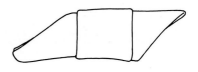

4. Fold in half to form the shape, as shown.

4. Gently take bottom point and curl under to form a ring.

4. Turn napkin over.

BISHOP'S HAT	PEACOCK'S TAIL	TUXEDO FOLD

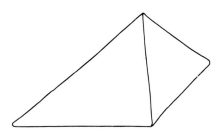

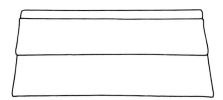

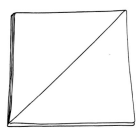

1. Fold diagonally to form a triangle; then fold both lower corners up to the center to form a diamond shape.

1. Fold down in half; fold top layer up to a point about 3 centimeters below the top edge.

1. Fold napkin into quarters, opening to the left; fold top flap diagonally to lower right corner.

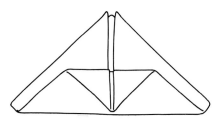

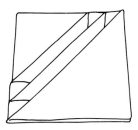

2. Fold the lower portion upwards, positioning the point about 3 centimeters below the top, and then fold tip back down on itself, as shown.

2. Similarly, fold lower layer under.

2. Fold next flap down and tuck into the pocket of the first fold, as shown; do the same with the next flap.

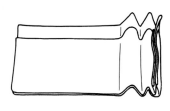

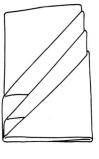

3. Turn the napkin over and fold one corner inside the other.

3. Fold in accordion pleats.

3. Fold right and left side under the napkin in thirds to form a rectangle.

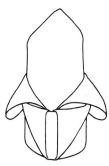

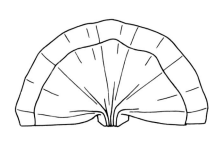

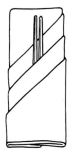

4. Turn over once more. Pull down the tips of the two top layers and tuck into the folds, as shown.

4. Open up as shown.

4. Insert chopsticks or cutlery.

BARON	ELEGANT FAN	JAPANESE FOLD

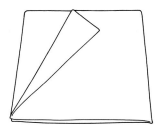

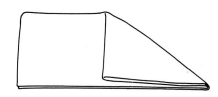

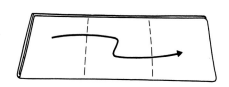

1. Fold napkin into quarters, opening to the left. Fold the top layer diagonally one quarter.

1. Fold napkin down, in half; bring upper right corner diagonally down to meet the center line.

1. In thirds, fold down the top edge and fold the bottom edge over. Lift the left edge and fold, as in a Z, into thirds.

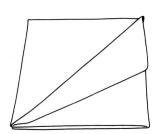

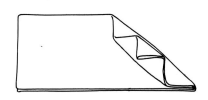

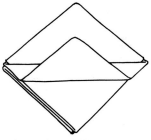

2. Fold the same flap over again.

2. Lift this flap and fold into thirds, as shown.

2. Rotate the napkin a half turn clockwise, fold the top layer down to meet the bottom, then turn it back on itself, as shown.

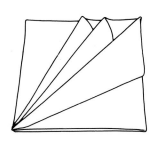

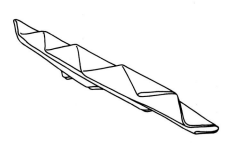

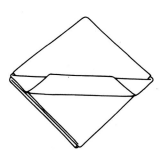

3. Fold the next layer down, as shown, and tuck into the pocket of the first fold; do the same with both remaining flaps.

3. Take the remainder of the napkin and fold into accordion pleats of the same width.

3. Insert this point into the pocket.

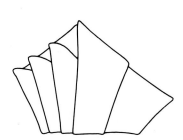

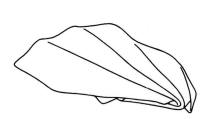

4. Fold bottom point under.

4. Fold about one third of the length of the right point under, as shown, then pull open top of napkin to create a fan effect.

4. Fold left and right corners under, as shown.

Balancing a tall flower arrangement with a figurine

A stone arch conversation piece

Opposite: A transparent objet *can afford to be tall*

TABLE ACCESSORIES

A wooden crane table accessory invokes good luck wishes

The term applies to anything set on the table besides table linens, cutlery, dinnerware, or glassware. Ordinarily, the category includes flowers, candles, salt and pepper shakers, and the like, but here we will confine our discussion to highly distinctive items made of china, glass, or metal, as well as valuable antiques and other *objets* which can serve as conversation pieces. Such accessories are particularly important in planning an unconventional, crossover setting; their presence enables dinner table conversation to flow freely, inspiring wide-ranging topics. Such conversation is itself the perfect exemplification of the crossover spirit.

Table accessories have much in common with the Japanese custom of placing objects in a *tokonoma*, or alcove, as room decoration. Objects on display silently convey a sense of the season, or of a special event; the very same principle can work on a table as well.

Certain basic rules apply to the use of accessories. First, height should be taken into consideration. As a rough guideline, place your elbow on the table and make a fist. Generally, accessories should not exceed the height of your fist. On the other hand, when a very tall accessory is desired, it should rise well above eye level. Second, combine different items. Rather than setting out a number of identical items, as with dinnerware, choose items of the same style but with different shapes to create a storyline. For example, when using T'ang figures of horses in three-color glaze, set horses all around the table in a variety of poses to create a single scene. Finally, think of the relationship between flowers and candles. Only when the *objets*, flowers, and candles are all arranged on the table is the composition of accessories complete. Subtle tensions and harmonies set up among the various items on the table can create an inspiring impression like that of listening to an orchestra, or viewing a multicolored painting.

Lending a Chinese touch: a Tang horse figure

Stimulating table conversation with antique salt and pepper shakers

Integrating cat figurines in a flower arrangement

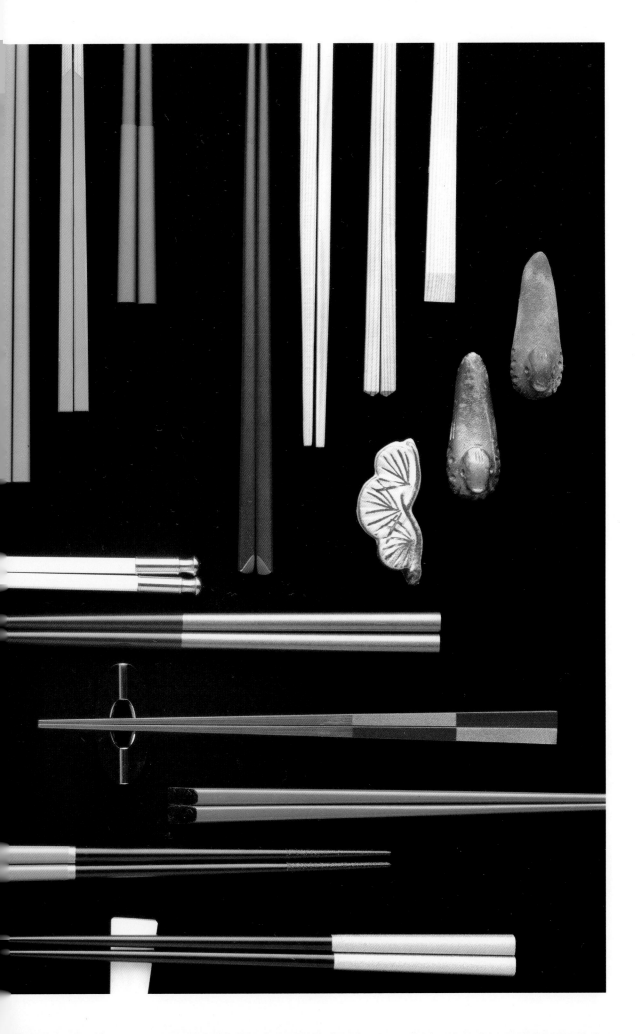

CHOPSTICKS AND CHOPSTICK RESTS

While many countries in the Eastern Asian region use chopsticks, including China, Japan, North and South Korea, Taiwan, and Vietnam, Japan is said to be the only country in the world where chopsticks are the sole traditional utensil for conveying food to the mouth. The other countries all use spoons along with chopsticks.

The precursor of modern chopsticks was a stick of bamboo bent into a tweezer shape in order to pick up food. Eventually, chopsticks evolved into their present shape of slender rods used in pairs to grasp and pick up food. They were introduced to Japan from China by Prince Shotoku (574–622), and now, some 1500 years later, they remain a fixture of daily life, used in cooking, serving, and eating, as well as in religious functions.

In China, chopsticks are used for rice and other solid foods, and spoons for soup. The chopsticks are long so that diners are able to serve themselves from large serving plates.

On the Korean peninsula, spoons are used for rice and soup, and chopsticks are used to pick up condiments and other foods. Korean chopsticks are often made of silver or stainless steel.

In Japan, there are many varieties of chopsticks, their use distinguished by materials and shape. To be able to differentiate among the varieties is a good way to increase the enjoyment of using chopsticks. The following is a summary of the types of chopsticks available and their traditional uses.

Bamboo chopsticks are used not only as individual eating implements but also as serving utensils. This is because bamboo will not absorb the oil, flavors, or aromas of the food. In very formal *kaiseki* cuisine, their use varies according to the position and shape of the nodes. Those with nodes near the top are used with raw foods, while those with nodes in the middle are used with vegetarian cuisine. Bamboo chopsticks with tapered ends and no nodes may be used for either type of food. These rules should best be adhered to on all *kaiseki*-like formal occasions.

Next are willow chopsticks. These implements, with tapered ends, are used on all formal occasions, such as at New Year celebrations and on other auspicious occasions.

Cedar chopsticks are fragrant, and so soft that they do not leave scratches on eating utensils. They are appropriate for casual occasions, and are widely used. Some say that cedar is beneficial for the health.

Lacquer chopsticks, being sturdy and easy to keep clean, are considered appropriate for home use, although at one time they were a luxury indulged in by wealthy merchants. They also receive high marks from an ecological standpoint, as they stand up well to frequent washings and can be used again and again.

If we turn to other countries, the list of materials can be expanded even further. Ivory chopsticks were once highly valued by royalty for their propensity to change color when exposed to poison. On the Korean peninsula and in Thailand, metal chopsticks are frequently used, primarily to serve food.

Chopstick rests have their own role to play. They are not used on formal occasions like the tea ceremony, but, rather, add a frequently whimsical element to a tablesetting, being much like tiny sculptures. Chopstick rests of unusual shape or material, or those conveying an especially strong sense of the season, can function as conversation pieces. Chopstick rests can also easily serve as rests for knives, forks, or spoons.

Materials for chopstick rests include every sort of natural material, from stone, bamboo, and lacquer to twigs of flowering cherry in spring. Again, rests made from ceramics should also be carefully selected, with the design appropriate to the season, if possible. Chinese meals often feature metal chopstick rests, usually of stainless steel or brass, which can be effective in creating an Oriental mood. Finally, the use of chopstick rests made of precious gems or ores, such as jadeite, can add depth to the tablesetting.

A floating candle

LIGHTING

When skillfully used according to the time, place, and purpose of the gathering, lighting can contribute greatly to the dramatic effect of the table.

Light can be divided broadly into artificial light and natural light. Natural light should be used in abundance. Should you find the afternoon sunshine attractive, as it is seen streaming through branches, or the twilight, when the sky casts a diffused lighting, then set the table by the window to take full advantage of it.

There are all sorts of artificial lighting, from torches and candles to oil lamps, incandescent lights, fluorescent lights, and laser beams. It is advisable to become familiar with the properties of each kind of light in order to gain the maximum benefit from it. The point is not to seek a close imitation of natural light, but rather to bring out and enjoy the special qualities of artificial light.

A modern candlestand in the midst of traditional Japanese ambience

Western lighting illuminates vertically

A symmetrical arrangement of Japanese-style lighting for a Western effect

Direct and indirect lightings are both appealing in their own ways, but for special crossover effects, indirect lighting is to be preferred. For example, in Byzantine-style architecture, a candle placed beside an openwork carving of arabesque design will produce the same design in shadow on the floor. Similarly, in Islamic architecture, sunlight streaming through a tiny stained-glass window can fill an entire room with a large replica of the stained glass design. Because indirect lighting is more common in Asian and Middle Eastern cultures, it can be used to evoke such an atmosphere. Gentle light filtering through a paper door; outdoor light creating shadows of trees and grasses on indoor walls; ground lights creating special highlights: All of these, and more, are effects of indirect lighting which can enhance a crossover occasion.

There are differences between Eastern and Western conventions in the use of light at mealtimes. In the West, light is considered something to place above the table; elevation of light, as through tall candelabra and overhead chandeliers, increases the beauty of Western dinnerware. In Japan, on the other hand, indirect light from a low angle is preferred. Gold or silver lacquer, as well as the rough texture of stoneware, gives off a mellow glow in soft, oblique, indirect light, creating an effect like that of shadow pictures.

Useful tools in creating special lighting effects include, first of all, candles.

These are distinguished by their color, height, thickness, fragrance, and type of flame. Of these qualities, height is of particular importance. If candle height is not in balance with the overall setting, the effectiveness of the candlelight is greatly diminished. Arranging a number of spherical or otherwise interestingly shaped candles can create a pleasing effect. French candles tend to be heavily perfumed, so beware. Japanese candles decorated with pretty designs also should not be forgotten.

Candles may be set in candlestands made of anything from silver to wood. In addition, they can be placed in piles of stones or *crudités*, and they can be set on mirrors or floated on water to double the flame. Set in cut glass, candles create wonderfully sparkling effects.

Candles set in a handcrafted paper lantern or simply placed behind an ornament made from handcrafted paper produce a Japanese atmosphere.

Oil lamps are another useful tool. They are distinguished by the color and fragrance of the oil, the thickness of the wick, and the design of the lamp. They are good for a casual occasion, and are especially evocative of Scandinavia.

Torches should be used boldly in outdoor garden parties, at the waterside, in the yard, or possibly on the approach to the main entrance.

A final word of advice: Do not be exclusively concerned with light itself, but seek ways to enjoy the effects of shadows as well.

A single lily gives a strong infusion of fragrance

FRAGRANCE

The fragrance of fruits for summer and autumn

In planning a tablesetting that appeals to all our senses, naturally fragrance must be brought into play. Since table odors touch on matters of etiquette, however, caution is advised.

Unpleasant odors must be avoided at all cost. These include stale room odors; overpowering fragrances of flowers at the table, such as lilies, daffodils, and eucalyptuses; offensive cooking odors; and strong perfumes.

On the other hand, agreeable smells, such as delicate, subtle incense, undeniably play a part in heightening people's appetites and uplifting their mood, so it is well worth seeking ways to incorporate fragrances without giving offense.

Among other points to be considered is the question of when to introduce fragrances to the table vicinity, whether before, during, or after the meal. A Chinese meal, for example, might begin with the fragrance of jasmine, followed by the bouquet of the food itself during the meal, and afterwards, the smell of mint. For a Japanese meal, simply burning incense before a meal can enhance the guests' pleasure. But during meals the smell should disappear.

Fragrances are of various kinds. First is the fragrance of flowers, which can be used to suggest the season; hyacinths, for example, announce the arrival of spring. Other desirable fragrances include droplets of fragrance oil on wood chips and those of potpourri and fruit, especially fruits with some tartness, such as lemon, lime, and apple. Oranges stuck with cloves and set on the table are doubly effective, being attractive as well as fragrant. Herbs may also be used, as by making a wreath of bay leaves.

Besides choosing the timing and variety of a fragrance for your tablesetting, feel free to improvise presentations: piling aromatic fruits in a large bowl, for example, or setting a lidded bowl on a console by the entrance, filled with an aromatic potpourri or scented wood chips. These, and many other ideas, can be easily carried out.

Finally, don't forget to use fragrances to convey a sense of the season. Incorporating traditional fragrances, such as lilies at Christmas time, incense at a Japanese seasonal festival in May, or other expressions of the season both East and West, is an excellent idea.

The subtle waft of incense

A large serving platter displays inviting morsels of food

A well-considered balance between tableware and color help to stimulate the appetite

Emphasizing the charm of small bottles of spirits

For large gatherings:
drama in a food presentation

Opposite: Japanese tea canisters hold
hors d'oeuvres at a cocktail party

SERVING

A little imagination in the serving of drinks, hors d'oeuvres, side dishes, or desserts can go a long way to create an enjoyable crossover effect. Hors d'oeuvres or desserts might be arranged on a single large serving platter. Unusual containers can serve as coolers for wine or champagne bottles. In addition to each person's individual placesetting, creating a focal point on the table to attract the attention of all heightens the drama of the dining space. For example, food might be placed in a five-tiered nest of lacquer boxes. The excitement of taking off the box lids will add greatly to the group's pleasure in the occasion. Arrange food on a beautiful platter with a pictorial design, or in a surprisingly unconventional dish. A large Japanese ceramic bowl may be used as a champagne cooler. These and many other ideas are possible to carry out without much difficulty. A traditional part of Japanese hospitality is to make the quality of the wares chosen an important part of the festivities. Treating one's guests not just to the food, but to the wares that contain it, is an important concept in a crossover tablesetting.

Finally, the most important point to remember in serving is the matter of timing. Coordination between serving and eating is a vital element in the success of a tablesetting.

SOURCES OF ORIENTAL TABLEWARE IN THE UNITED STATES AND CANADA

Following is a list of retail establishments and galleries where examples of Oriental materials and objects mentioned in this book may be found.

ARIZONA

Orient East
6204 North Scottsdale Road
(Lincoln Village Shops)
Scottsdale 85253
(602) 948-0489
Furnishings, artifacts

CALIFORNIA

Abacus
1012 Alma Street
Menlo Park 94025
(415) 323-5893
Antiques, folkcraft

Asakichi
1730 Geary Boulevard
San Francisco 94115
(415) 921-2147
Furniture, porcelain, Japanese accessories

Roger Barber
114 Pine Street
San Anselmo 94960
(415) 457-6844
Antiques

Elaine Barchan Interiors
2261 Highland Oaks Drive
Arcadia 91006
By appointment
Antique textiles

Robert Brian Co.
Galleria/Design Center
101 Henry Adams, Space 136
San Francisco 94103
(415) 621-2273
Wide selection of antiques and folkcraft
Principally wholesale.

Bunka-Do
340 East 1st Street
Los Angeles 90012
(213) 625-8673
Folkcraft, ceramics

Arlene Cox Textiles
750 Adella Avenue
Coronado 92118
(619) 435-3054
By appointment
Antique, *mingei*, textiles

The Crane and Turtle
2550 California Street
San Francisco 94115
(415) 567-7383
Wide collection of fine & folk art, antique and contemporary

Den Japanese Art Salon
444 South Flower Street
Los Angeles 90017
(213) 489-1508
Changing exhibition of traditional crafts presented by Japan Center for Traditional Crafts, Tokyo

Elica's Paper
1801 4th Street
Berkeley 94710
(415) 845-9530
Washi—wide selection of handcrafted paper

Dodi Fromson
P.O. Box 49808
Los Angeles 90049
(213) 451-1110
By appointment
Antiques, textiles, metalwork, lacquerware

Fumiki Fine Arts
2001 Union Street
San Francisco 94123
(415) 922-0573
Porcelain

Genji
501 York Street
San Francisco 94110
(415) 255-2215
    and
1731 Buchanan Street
San Francisco 94115
(415) 931-1616
Wide selection of folk art

Gump's
250 Post Street
San Francisco 94108
(415) 982-1616
800-652-1662 dialing within Ca.
800-227-3135 from out of state
    and
9560 Wilshire Boulevard
Beverly Hills 92000
(213) 278-3200
Wide collection of antiques, furniture and art objects

Hayashi Oriental Antiques
1894 Union Street
San Francisco 94123

Habitat
158 East Tahquitz-McCallum Way
Palm Springs 92262
(619) 325-4042
Antique porcelain

Japan Gallery
2624 Wilshire Boulevard
Santa Monica 90403
(213) 453-6406
Baskets

Japan Interiors
1840 Fulton Avenue
Sacramento 95825
(916) 486-1251
Shoji, tatami, gifts

The Japan Trading Co.
1762 Buchanan Street
San Francisco 94115
(415) 929-0989
Shoji, tatami

Japonesque
50 Post Street
Crocker Center Galleria, 54
San Francisco 94104
(415) 398-8577
Wide selection of antique and contemporary home furnishings

Kasuri Dye-Works
1959 Shattuck Avenue
Berkeley 94704
(415) 841-4509
Kasuri, silk, *yukata* fabric by the yard, wooden folkcrafts.
Mail order video available

Kinokuniya Stationery & Gift
Suite #218
Japan Center, Kinokuniya Bldg.
1581 Webster Street
San Francisco 94115
(415) 567-8901
Washi

Kogura Company
231 East Jackson Street
San Jose 95112
(408) 264-3184
Chinaware

Komoto Department Store
1528 Kern Street
Fresno 93706
(209) 268-6502
Chinaware, baskets, textiles

Kuromatsu
722 Bay Street
San Francisco 94109
(415) 474-4027
Antiques, *mingei*

Marukyo U.S.A.
New Otani Hotel Arcade
110 South Los Angeles Street
Los Angeles 90012
(213) 628-4369
Fabrics

McMullen's Japanese Antiques
146 North Robertson Boulevard
Los Angeles 90048
(213) 652-9492
and
1615 Stanford Street
Santa Monica 90404
(213) 828-7479
(213) 828-3032
Folk art, lacquerware, porcelain, ceramics

Mikado (J. C. Trading, Inc.)
1737 Post Street
San Francisco 94115
(415) 922-9450
Interior decorations

Mingei International Museum of World Folk Art
4405 La Jolla Village Drive, Bldg. 1-7
San Diego 92122
(619) 453-5300

Nichi Bei Bussan
1715 Buchanan Mall
San Francisco 94115
(415) 346-2117
and
140 Jackson Street
San Jose 95112
(408) 294-8048
Folk art, fabrics by the yard

Nikaku Japanese Art
615 North 6th Street
San Jose 95112
(408) 971-2822
Wide selection of folkcraft

Oriental Arts
1206 Orange Avenue
Coronado 92118
(619) 435-5451
Lacquerware, porcelain

Oriental Corner
280 Main Street
Los Altos 94022
(415) 941-3207
Lacquerware, porcelain

Oriental Porcelain Gallery
2702 Hyde Street
San Francisco 94109
(415) 776-5969
Antique porcelain

Oriental Treasure Box
Olde Cracker Factory
Antique Shopping Center
448 West Market Street
San Diego 92101
(619) 233-3831
Lacquerware, folk art, porcelain, textiles,
hibachi

Orientations
34 Maiden Lane
San Francisco 94108
(415) 981-3972
and
189 North Robertson Boulevard
Beverly Hills 90212
(213) 659-7431
Porcelain, baskets, screens

Pacific Asia Museum
46 North Los Robles Avenue
Pasadena 91101
(818) 449-2742

Rafu Bussan, Inc.
326 East 2nd Street
Los Angeles 90012
(213) 626-3970
Chinaware, lacquerware

Sakura Horikiri
Tozai Plaza
15480 South Western Av.
Gardena, 90249
(213) 323-1821
Washi

Sanko Cooking Supply Company
1758 Buchanan Mall
San Francisco 94115
(415) 922-8331
Chinaware, lacquerware

Soko Hardware
1698 Post Street
San Francisco 94115
(415) 931-5510
Porcelain, chopstick rests

Soko Interiors
1672 Post Street
San Francisco 94115
(415) 922-4155
Folkcraft, furniture, lacquerware, porcelain

Takahashi Oriental Decor
235 15th Street
San Francisco 94103
(415) 552-5511
Wide selection of textiles, screens, furnishings,
folkcraft, ceramics

Takahashi Trading Corp.
200 Rhode Island Street
San Francisco 94103
(415) 431-8300
Screens, *shoji*

Tansu Collections
Box 1396
Menlo Park 94025
(415) 323-6272
By appointment
Textiles, *mingei*, customized furniture

Tokyo Gift Shop
Lincoln and Ocean Avenue
Carmel 93921
(408) 624-3646
Antique porcelain, screens,
furniture

Townhouse Living
1825 Post Street
San Francisco 94115
(415) 568-1417
Folkcraft, furniture

The Yorozu
2615 Riverside Boulevard
Sacramento 95818
(916) 442-8631
Chinaware, lacquerware, baskets, textiles

The Zentner Collection
5757 Landregan Street
Emeryville 94608
(415) 653-5181
Very large selection of antiques,
especially *mingei*

COLORADO

Kobun-sha
Sakura Square
1255 19th Street
Denver 80202
(303) 295-1856
Home furnishings, lacquerware

CONNECTICUT

The Kura
310 Rockrimmon Road
Stamford 06903
(203) 329-1778
By appointment
Hibachi, baskets, screens

Midori
7 Campbell Drive
Stamford 06903
(203) 322-3205
By appointment
Wide variety of antiques & folkcraft
including Imari

Vallin Galleries
516 Danbury Road (Rte. 7)
Wilton 06897
(203) 762-7441
Fine porcelain, *hibachi*,
stone lanterns, art

DISTRICT OF COLUMBIA

Arise Gallery
6295 Willow Street, N.W.
Washington, D.C. 20012
(202) 291-0770
Hibachi, screens, baskets, porcelain

Asian Art Center
2709 Woodley Pl., N.W.
Washington, D.C. 20008
(202) 234-3333
Porcelain, lacquerware, screens

Ginza
1721 Connecticut Avenue, N.W.
Washington, D.C. 20008
(202) 331-7991
Folk art, porcelain, crafts

Harding-Giannini Antiques
Tenjin-san, Inc.
1083 Wisconsin Avenue, N.W.
Washington, D.C. 20007
(202) 333-5999
Ceramics, textiles, folkcraft

FLORIDA

Harper Galleries / Bijutsu, Inc.
333 Worth Avenue
Palm Beach, 33480
(407) 655-8490
Traditional furnishings,
art, accessories

Palm Beach Interiors Inc.
309 Peruvian Avenue
Palm Beach 33480
(407) 832-3461
Antique porcelain, paintings, furniture

GEORGIA

Art Gallery Colony Square
1197 Peachtree Street, N.E.
Atlanta 30361
(404) 261-1233
Arts, crafts

HAWAII

Bushido
936 Maunakea Street
Honolulu 96817
(808) 536-5693
Fax: (808) 521-1994
Ceramics

Garakuta-do
444 Hobron Lane
Honolulu 96815
(808) 955-2099
    and
938 Maunakea Street
Honolulu 96817
(808) 536-5786
Imari, *mingei*, textiles

Mills Gallery
701 Bishop Street
Honolulu 96815
(808) 536-3527
Antiques, folkcraft, interior design

ILLINOIS

Aiko's Art Materials
3347 North Clark Street
Chicago 60657
(312) 404-5600
Washi, contemporary Japanese prints

Kiyo's Inc.
2831 North Clark Street
Chicago 60657
(312) 935-0619
Chinaware

Saito Inc.
Suite 410
840 North Michigan Avenue
Chicago 60611
(312) 642-4366
By appointment
Porcelain, lacquerware

J. Toguri Mercantile Co.
851 West Belmont Avenue
Chicago 60657
(312) 929-3500
Home furnishings, lacquerware

KENTUCKY

Boones Antiques
4996 Old Versailles Road
Lexington 40504
(606) 254-5335
Porcelain, furniture

Wakefield-Scearce
525 Washington Street
Shelbyville 40065
(502) 633-4382
Porcelain

LOUISIANA

Oriental Art and Antiques of Diane Genre
233 Royal Street
New Orleans 70130
(504) 525-7270
Antiques, screens, furniture, prints, textiles,
lacquerware

MAINE

Barbara Forlano
P.O. Box 462
Chases Pond Road
York 03909
(207) 363-7009
Porcelain

MARYLAND

Knight-Flight
P.O. Box 2518
Gaithersburg 20886
(301) 921-0386
Ceramics, furniture, textiles,
woodblock prints

MASSACHUSETTS

Alberts-Langdon, Inc.
126 Charles Street
Boston 02114
(617) 523-5954
Furniture, porcelain

Bernheimer's Antique Arts
52-C Brattle Street
Cambridge 02138
(617) 547-1117
Ceramics, prints, *mingei*

Dynasty Gallery
377 Route 20
Sudbury 01776
(508) 443-5573
    and
1033 Massachusetts Avenue
Cambridge 02138
(617) 864-8449
Furniture, lamps, *hibachi*,
porcelain, artwork

Eastern Accent
237 Newbury Street
Boston 02116
(617) 266-9707
Contemporary, handcrafted designs for
dining and the home.
Catalog available

Robert C. Eldred Co., Inc.
1483 Route 6A
East Dennis 02641
(508) 385-3116
Wide selection of antiques, arts,
accessories

Vilunya Folk Art
Vilunya Diskin
Charles Square 5 Bennett Street
Cambridge 02138
(617) 661-5753
Folkcraft, lacquerware

MISSOURI

Asiatica Ltd.
205 Westport Road
Kansas City 64111
(816) 931-9111
Furniture, textiles, *mingei*

Brookside Antiques
6219 Oak Street
Kansas City 64113
(816) 444-4774
Furniture, porcelain

NEW HAMPSHIRE

The Garakuta Collection
65 Bow Street
Portsmouth 03801
(603) 433-1233 or 964-9241
Antiques and contemporary objects—*mingei*,
textiles

NEW JERSEY

Ivory Bird
555 Bloomfield Avenue
Montclair 07000
(201) 744-5225
Imari, prints

NEW MEXICO

Mary Hunt Kahlenberg
1571 Canyon Road
Santa Fe 87501
(505) 983-9780
By appointment
Textile, arts

Little Shop
Water Street Plaza
138 West Water Street
Santa Fe 87501
(505) 984-1050
Fine art

NEW YORK

Art Asia, Inc.
1088 Madison Avenue (81st Street)
New York City 10028
(212) 249-7250
Lacquerware, porcelain, baskets, furniture

Asia Society
725 Park Avenue
New York City 10021
(212) 288-6400
Keyaki stationery boxes, ironware
teapots, ceremonial teacups—Shino ware

Azuma International
251 East 86th Street
New York City 10028
(212) 369-4928
Home furnishings

Azuma Lexington Avenue
666 Lexington Avenue
New York City 10022
(212) 752-0599
Home furnishings

Azuma Village
25 West 8th Street
New York City 10003
(212) 673-2900
Home furnishings

Azuma West
387 Sixth Avenue
New York City 10014
(212) 989-8960
Home furnishings

Crestwood
315 Hudson Street
New York City 10013
(212) 989-2700
Toll Free: 800-344-2692
Fax: (212) 929-7532
Largest importer of Oriental papers

Daikichi
Madison Street
Sag Harbor 11963
(516) 725-1533
In Manhattan by appointment:
(212) 532-2192
Wide variety of furnishings, textiles

Eastern Dreams
6 Greenridge Drive
Chappaqua 10514
(914) 666-8910
By appointment
Porcelain, lacquerware, paper and wood crafts,
ikebana planters, contemporary screens

Edo Antiques Ltd.
67 East 11th Street
New York City 11011
(212) 254-2508
Furniture, porcelain, art

80 Papers
510 Broome Street
New York City
(212) 431-7720
Washi

Five Eggs
436 West Broadway
New York City 10012
(212) 226-1606
Antiques, ceramics, *mingei, tatami*

Flying Cranes Antiques
Manhattan Art & Antique Center
1050 2nd Avenue (56th Street)
New York City 10022
(212) 223-4600
Antiques—Imari, silver

Gordon Foster Antiques
1322 3rd Avenue (75th Street)
New York City 10021
(212) 744-4922
Mingei, baskets, ceramics, porcelain

Charles R. Gracie & Sons, Inc.
979 3rd Avenue
New York City 10022
(212) 753-5350
Hibachi, screens

Japanese Screen
23-37 91st Street
East Elmhurst 11369
(718) 803-2267
Shoji, tatami, lamps

John Rogers
63 Main Street
Southampton 11968
(516) 283-0715
Lacquerware, housewares

Jomon Gallery
550 Madison Avenue (55th Street)
New York City 10022
(212) 935-1089
Fine traditional craftwork

Katagiri & Co., Inc.
Seikatsukan
226 East 59th Street
New York City 10022
(212) 752-4197
Mingei, lacquerware, porcelain

Kate's Paperie
8 West 13th Street
New York City 10011
(212) 633-0570
Wide selection of *washi*

Kimono House
120 Thompson Street
New York City 10012
(212) 966-5939
Antique kimono and small items

Koto
71 West Houston Street
New York City 10012
(212) 533-8601
Lacquerware, screens, contemporary
ceramics, crafts

Leighton R. Longhi
P.O. Box 6704
New York City 10128
Fax: (212) 996-0721
Museum quality fine art

Meijiya Trading Co.
2642 Central Park Avenue
Yonkers 10710
(914) 961-1257
Chinaware

Metropolitan Museum of Art
5th Avenue at 82nd Street
New York City 10028
(212) 879-5500
Gift shop: lacquerware, ceramics

Miya Shoji & Interiors, Inc.
109 West 17th Street
New York City 10011
(212) 243-6774
Japanese rooms. *shoji*, light fixtures,
stone lanterns

Naga Antiques Ltd.
145 East 61st Street
New York City 10021
(212) 593-2788
Sculpture, ceramics, furniture, lacquerware,
screens

New York Kinokuniya Bookstore
10 West 49th Street at Rockefeller Plaza
New York City 10020
(212) 765-1461
Washi

Orientations Gallery
Place des Antiquaires
Gallery Twenty-two
125 East 57th Street
New York City 10022
(212) 371-9006
Antique lacquerware

Pillow Perfections
12 Stuyvesant Street
New York City 10003
(212) 528-5183
Tatami

Ronin Gallery
605 Madison Avenue
New York City 10022
(212) 688-0188
Ceramics, baskets

Talas
213 West 35th Street
New York City
(212) 736-7744
Washi

Tansuya Corp.
159 Mercer Street
New York City 10012
(212) 966-1782
Furniture, screens, lacquerware

Things Japanese
1109 Lexington Avenue (2nd fl.)
New York City 10021
(212) 249-3591
Mingei, baskets, Imari, furniture

Tokyo Arts Salon
Manhattan Art & Antique Center
1050 2nd Avenue (56th Street)
New York City 10022
(212) 888-7195
Antique Imari

Tsuru Gallery
22 East 66th Street
New York City 10021
(212) 772-6422
Screens

Joanne Wise
The Wise Collection
4 Morningside Circle
Bronxville 10708
(914) 961-9325
Contemporary ceramics, artwork,
sculpture

Zen Oriental Bookstore
521 5th Avenue
New York City 10017
(212) 697-0840
Washi, ceramics

OHIO

Mary Baskett Gallery
1002 St. Gregory Street
Cincinnati 45202
(513) 421-0460
Ceramics, Oriental art

Ginkgo Tree
Dillonvale Shopping Center
4389 East Galbraith Road
Deerpark, Cincinnati
(513) 984-0553
Ceramics, porcelain

Mitzie Verne Collection
John Carroll University
The Grasselli Library Gallery
20700 North Park Boulevard
University Heights 44118
(216) 397-4551
Mail to: 3326 Lansmere Road
Shaker Heights 44122
Screens, contemporary ceramics

OREGON

Nelson & Yoshizu Antiques
521 Southwest 11th Avenue
Portland 45770
(503) 228-4436
Antiques, art

Shibumi Trading Ltd.
P.O. Box 1-F
Eugene 97440
Outside of Oregon:
1-800-843-2565
In Oregon: (503) 683-1331
Stone lanterns, basins, wide selection
of folkcraft
Mail order catalog available.

Shogun's Gallery
206 Northwest 23rd Avenue
Portland 97210
(503) 224-0328
Mingei, textiles, porcelain

PENNSYLVANIA

Pearl of the East
Willow Grove Park
Springfield Mall
1615 Walnut Street
Philadelphia 19100
(215) 563-1563
Furnishings, porcelain

Sanctuary Futon Co.
217 Church Street
Philadelphia 19106
(215) 925-9460
Tatami

Three Cranes Gallery
18-20 Mechanic Street
New Hope 18938
(215) 862-5626
Porcelain, textiles, prints, *shoji*, *tatami*

RHODE ISLAND

Norton's Oriental Gallery
415 Thames Street
Newport 02840
(401) 849-4468
Antiques

Oriental Arts Ltd.
Brickmarket Place
Newport 02840
(401) 846-0655
Antiques, reproductions, accessories,
furniture

SOUTH CAROLINA

The Red Torii
197 King Street
Charleston 29401
(803) 723-0443
Porcelain

TEXAS

East & Orient Co.
2901 North Henderson
Dallas 75206
(214) 826-1191
Fax: (214) 821-8632
Porcelain, lacquerware, screens

Gump's
The Galleria, Suite 1105
13350 Dallas Parkway
Dallas 75240
(214) 392-0200
Antiques, lanterns, screens

Janet Lashbrooke Oriental Antiques
112 Sugarberry Circle
Houston 77024
(713) 953-9144
Mingei, baskets, teapots

Loyd-Paxton, Inc.
3636 Maple Avenue
Dallas 75219
(214) 521-1521
Textiles, lacquerware, screens, porcelain,
bronzes

Translations
4811 Abbott
Dallas 75205
(214) 522-1115, 351-0285
By appointment
Home accessories

WASHINGTON

Asia Gallery
1220 1st Avenue
Seattle 98101
(206) 622-0516
Wide selection of antiques, folkcraft, including
textiles, furniture, baskets, porcelain

Honeychurch Antiques Ltd.
1008 James Street
Seattle 98104
(206) 622-1225
Furniture, ceramics, sculptures

Japanese Antiquities Gallery
200 East Boston Street
Seattle 98102
(206) 324-3322
Antique folk art, furniture,
ceramics

Kagedo
55 Spring Street
Seattle 98104
(206) 467-9077
and
1100 Western Avenue
Seattle 98101
(206) 467-5847
Antiques, folk art

Marvel on Madison
69 Madison
Seattle 98104
(206) 624-4225
Folk crafts, ceramics, lacquerware

Uwajimaya
6th Avenue South and South King Street
Seattle 98104
(206) 624-6248
Washi, shoji lamps, *ikebana* vases

CANADA

TORONTO

Dolly Beil Ltd.
986 Eglinton Avenue, West
Toronto, Ontario M6C 2C5
(416) 781-2334
Kutani & Satsuma porcelain

Gallery Shioda
98 Avenue Road
Toronto, Ontario M5R 2H3
(416) 961-2066
Wide selection of antiques

Japanese Paper Place
966 Queen Street, West
Toronto, Ontario M6J 1G8
(416) 533-6862
Washi, including *shoji*, stencilled paper,
origami paper

Okame Japanese Antiques
709 Devonshire Road
Windsor, Ontario N8Y 2L9
(519) 254-4363
By appointment
Ceramics, baskets, scrolls,
metalwork, folk art

VANCOUVER

Japanese Accents Kiku
1532 Marine Drive
West Vancouver, B.C. V7V 1H8
(604) 925-2584
Chabako, mingei, textiles, ceramics

Potter's Gallery
665 Howe Street
Vancouver, B.C. V6C 2E5
(604) 685-3919
Imari, Satsuma, Kutani

Dorian Rae Collection
3151 Granville Street
Vancouver, B.C. V6H 3K1
(604) 732-6100
and
2033 West 4th Avenue
Vancouver
(604) 732-6100
Screens, ceramics, *hibachi*

Frankie Robinson Oriental Gallery
3055 Granville Street
Vancouver, B.C. V6H 3J9
(604) 734-6568
Mingei, Satsuma, *hibachi*, screens